AGELESS

Think Young and Live Younger

SABRINA PROTIC

Copyright © 2019 by NOW SC Press

All rights reserved. No part of this publication may be reproduced, distributed, or transmitted in any form or by any means, including photocopying, recording, or other electronic or mechanical methods, without the prior written permission of the publisher, except in the case of brief quotations embodied in critical reviews and certain other noncommercial uses permitted by copyright law. For permission requests, write to the publisher, addressed "Attention: Permissions Coordinator," via the website below.

1.888.5069-NOW
www.nowscpress.com
@nowscpress

Ordering Information:

Quantity sales. Special discounts are available on quantity purchases by corporations, associations, and others. For details, contact the publisher at the address above.

Orders by U.S. trade bookstores and wholesalers. Please contact: NOW SC Press: Tel: (888) 5069-NOW or visit www.PublishWithNOW.com.

Printed in the United States of America

First Printing, 2019

ISBN: 978-1-7341809-1-6

Dedication

This book is dedicated to my husband for supporting me along the way and to my mother for knowing the way, living the way, and showing me the way to purposeful fulfillment.

Contents

Foreword 1
Introduction 3

Part One: Mindset Makeover 5
    Chapter 1: My Life is ~~Over~~ Just Beginning 7
    Chapter 2: I'm a ~~Failure~~ Success 15
    Chapter 3: I Have ~~No Worth~~ So Much Worth 23

Part Two: Self Makeover 33
    Chapter 4: I Like ~~Being Alone~~ Building Connections ... 35
    Chapter 5: ~~I'm Afraid~~ I'm Taking Chances 45
    Chapter 6: I Like ~~Predictability~~ Disrupting the Routine ... 53
    Chapter 7: I Have ~~No~~ Tons of Energy 63

Part Three: Body Makeover 71
    Chapter 8: I'm ~~out of~~ In Shape 73
    Chapter 9: I'm ~~on a Diet~~ Living Healthy 83
    Chapter 10: The All-Over Make Over 93

About Women's Entrepreneurial Empowerment (W.E.E.) 103
About the Author 109

Foreword

When I was introduced to Sabrina, she was as classy and sassy as anyone I'd met along my journey. I immediately fell in love with her energy, her enthusiasm, and her authenticity. She was the real deal.

No surprise, then, that her first book (I hope there are many more) is as strong as she is.

Now I can see that her strength came at a price. She learned how to turn stumbling blocks into stepping stones one day, one thought at a time. She was willing to pay the price of patience and perseverance because her vision of her true ageless self was so clear.

Sabrina's journey from a talented and confident teenager, to losing herself, to her relationships, is one I have seen hundreds of times in my years of coaching. It's my story too. What stood out for me as I read her words was how her indomitable spirit kept shining through, coaxing her to take huge risks in the midst of her greatest darkness and deepest despair.

Sabrina didn't have a knight in shining armor to rescue her. She saved herself, and shows us how it's done. I shared this book with a friend the day after I read it and remember our conversation the next evening on the phone:

"'When I got up this morning and started reading, I couldn't put it down, but I had to go to work, so I finished it over lunch. I love her voice, and I really needed her message. Thank you so much for sharing it with me, MK. It is definitely a book that deserves 5 stars!"

I am so grateful for this ageless, timeless wisdom, and for befriending the shining light that is its author. Sabrina does deserve 5 stars, and by the end of this book, you'll see that you do, too.

Instead of growing older, we can grow bolder when we keep growing. My hope is that as you hear Sabrina's struggles and successes, you'll realize you're not alone. And that as you follow her gentle but firm guidance, you'll discover and celebrate an ageless and limitless You.

In joy,

MK Mueller

Author of *Taking Care of Me: The Habits of Happiness* and *8 to Great: The Powerful Process of Positive Change*

Introduction

There's that one mirror moment in everyone's life when you realize the reflection you are seeing looks, feels, and thinks differently from years before. You wonder, when and how did this happen? Sometimes the answer is a traumatic change in circumstances, like divorce, health issues, employment dilemmas, or the acceleration of aging. If that is you in the mirror, then this book is your wakeup call! It's time to slow down the freight train that ages you mentally and physically.

There's so much mental energy that impacts how you look and feel. Have you sometimes felt that your life was over or that you are a failure and have no self-worth? Finding your way back from that can be a challenge and can leave a trail of damage behind from the dark days you went through. In this book, I will show you how you can and will find your way not just back, but to an even better place. A simple shift in your mindset followed by a few actionable steps can make a big difference.

Growing Ageless discusses in detail how we all go through a downward spiral in life because of the road bumps we hit along the way, and gives you concrete strategies for how to create a new, revitalized you! I will give you the roadmap to reconnect with people, develop new interests, and disrupt the predictable routines in your life. This book discusses my secrets to help you ramp up your energy, shape up your physique, and enjoy a healthier, ageless lifestyle. Come along with me on this life-changing journey!

Sabrina Protic

Part One

MINDSET MAKEOVER

Chapter 1

My Life is ~~Over~~ Just Beginning

The day my divorce was stamped FINAL, I remember standing outside the courthouse and thinking, *my life is over.* All around me, people were moving about their lives, hurrying to jobs and families and success, while I stood in the sun and wondered who I was now that I was no longer half of someone else.

How Did I Get Here?

Twenty years earlier, I'd stood in the sun in a custom-made wedding gown with three hundred handsewn pearls trailing along the bodice, and pledged to love this man for the rest of my life. We did what you are supposed to do—bought a car and a house, and with it, we thought, the keys to happiness. We fell into a routine: regular spiritual worship, building our careers, hanging out with friends, and staying physically fit. While I was growing up, my mother always encouraged me to take care of my body, hair, and skin, and that was something that I continued to do throughout my married life.

We had two children, got a dog, and lived the picture-perfect suburban life. All the while, I felt the pressure of juggling full-time work with being a wife and mother, as well as chief dog mom and sole housekeeper. Maybe I did all of that because of the nurturing instinct a woman has, to take care of anything breathing that comes into the home.

The Cost of Self-Sacrifice

However, all this came at the cost of my identity. My energies went in every direction—making sure the laundry was done, homework completed, meals cooked, house clean, social calendars filled—every direction but into what I needed. I sensed there was something lacking, some need deep inside myself, so I decided to go back to school and get my college degree. The juggling act only got more difficult when I added school into the mix, but I did it, graduating four years later, with my children sitting in the audience beaming with joy and happiness.

I was smiling too, but inside, I wondered if my life was already over. Six months earlier, the divorce had been finalized and I was now a statistic: A mid-life divorcee with children. I stood on that stage, clutching my diploma, feeling empty, lost, and alone.

Mourning What Was and Won't Be

The next five years of my life were spent in a cycle of despair and emptiness. My friends, who had been "couple friends" with me and my husband, struggled to decide who to include in their circle of activities. Others chose a villain in the breakup and ostracized one of us to maintain the friendship with the other. As I withdrew more and more, the invitations to join parties, attend events or to just hang out stopped coming. I sunk into a deep depression. For three years, I wore nothing but black from head to toe. My co-workers would tease me about always wearing black, but I couldn't seem to add any color to my life or to myself. In my head, wearing black made me look thinner and more invisible, and in those dark days, all I wanted was to disappear.

I felt old, ugly, and unwanted. Walking around with my head down made me feel less noticed. I couldn't accept a compliment and couldn't believe I would find love again, never mind date. How could I compete with the thin, fit women in their twenties and thirties? Who was going to want me, a woman in her late forties with two children?

My life narrowed and narrowed until all I did was maintain my spiritual routine, taxi the teenagers around, go to work and once in a while go to the movies alone. There were many times that I cried during those movies as I sat and watched someone else's happy ending unfold on the screen. In the dark, no one could see my self-pity and loneliness.

The Shift in Thinking

The one good thing I did for myself was something my mother encouraged me to do. We booked an eleven-day trip to Hawaii, financing this dream trip to all three islands. A family friend agreed to take care of my children while I was away. My heart was pounding and my palms were sweaty as I boarded the ship knowing I was leaving my children behind. But as the ship pulled away from the dock, I began to feel more and more like the woman I used to be when I was young. My mother filled in the gaps for the relationships I had yet to form, becoming my champion and my stronghold. She encouraged me to stretch my wings and try everything the cruise ship offered—dance classes, art gallery exhibits, offshore adventures and musical performances. The trip was divine, a pocket of light that gave me hope for the future. I had taken a bold step forward, with this first trip just for me, and that meant I could take another step, and another.

Things began to change, in tiny ways, after I got home. A friend of mine from the past relocated back to my hometown and reconnected with me. Right away, she invited me to a girl's night at someone's home. It was my first outing in a group setting, which scared me a lot. I was so afraid someone would ask me about my life and my divorce—AKA my failure, at least in my mind. I will never forget that night when we all sat in a circle and everyone had to share a little bit about themselves. My heart was pounding a thousand beats per minute when it was my turn.

> **ONE THING TO DO TODAY**
>
> Because women often have massive To Do lists, I want you to just do one thing today. It's a simple one, but it can change your life. Today, adopt a new message of mental affirmation: *It is time for me to add life back into my life.*

The only thing I could say was my name. I had nothing else to add. I realized in that moment that I had allowed myself to completely disconnect from life. These ladies were so kind to me, giving me that moment to pause and think, before eventually circling back around to me. They drew me out with simple, easy-to-answer questions. One word after another, I began reconnecting with people, interacting with other women who were so much like me, and becoming engaged in conversation. At the end of the evening I felt life coming back to me. Not only had I opened up and breathed life into myself, but I also then shifted more of my attention to the other ladies and helped to breathe life into them by supporting their lives, passions and stories. It is my hope that my midlife mindset journey will help you reset your thinking to a better place.

Most of all, I realized one vitally important, life-changing fact: *I was not alone.*

The Importance of Others

Years earlier when I stood on those courthouse steps, I felt embarrassed, like I had somehow failed at the one thing I was expected to do. Because of that, I lost myself and began to retreat from my life. While I sat there in a stranger's living room and listened to those other women, I heard a common thread—getting older, feeling lost and disconnected, needing to restore a sense of self. That common bond encouraged me to reach out and in turn, work on my own life and self.

That shift in thinking changed everything. It gave me a mental clarity that helped me make the shift from the depths of depression to a journey of ageless redirection, with hope, purpose, and vitality.

It was like someone turned on a light in my brain: *My life was not over, it was just beginning, and the only aging I was doing was in my head.* I started my ageless journey by recognizing the need to make internal and external changes, beginning with my wardrobe. Piece by piece, I replaced all the black in my closet with color. I joined a gym. I began to form friendships and go out with the girls.

A new me needed to break through the walls that I had built, but it had to start with my mind. I needed a midlife mindset reboot. Even as my body got toned, and my health improved, I had to work on the thoughts in my head. Living that empty, lonely life made me look, feel, think, and act older. To become truly ageless, I had to realize I was not a failure. Getting divorced was a stage in my life, not an ending.

Success is How You Define It

Society defines success with white picket fences and diamond rings. If you let the world give you a definition, you'll forever chase an impossible goal. Losing a job, getting divorced, starting over in any way is not a failure. It's a turn onto a new road.

That new road can lead to an eternal and rewarding ageless persona. Finding yourself, accepting yourself as you are right this minute, and then choosing to live the best you, regardless of your age and circumstances is the start. You are never too old, too tired, or too anything to find happiness and fulfillment. You aren't competing with younger men or women—you are battling your own mind and mistaken thoughts. We must all take ownership of our status and stature in life by the way we choose to exist. Those choices include shifting to an empowered mindset, wellness, fitness, dress, grooming, and diet.

Agelessness Attracts Others

The laws of attraction support ageless living and will open the doors for people who want to be around you, and thus expand the agelessness to them as well. As my thinking changed, so did my circle. My current husband said he noticed me because I looked like I was having tons of fun. We hung out together with mutual friends and before long, we were hooked on each other. We were in our fifties, yet acting twenty years younger.

It's never too late to live your best life and be your best you. Start right this very moment and make small changes in your life, your thinking, your outlook, your appearance, and your perception of yourself. Agelessness will come, and so will joy and a renewed sense of self. This book is about tiny redirections that every single one of us can do. Today, stop thinking your life is over because you are _____ (fill in the blank with whatever negative thought you have right now).

Instead, change those thoughts to reinforce that your life is just beginning. Say that to yourself right now: "My life is just beginning." Say it again. A third time. Say it until you believe it.

The Mirror Moment

At the end of every chapter, we will have a Mirror Moment, which is a self-examination question to think about. When we look in the mirror, we see all of our imperfections, blemishes, lines, wrinkles, and flaws. We focus on the things we need to fix, not the things that are already beautiful and perfect, and worth celebrating. Or we ignore the very things we need to change in order to live our best lives. So today, I want you to look in the mirror and ask yourself this:

Have I allowed myself to think that my usefulness, purpose and value are over?

If you have, then let's change that. Let's start by rewriting the thoughts in your head, and crossing out the thinking that leads to a loss of joy and purpose. Your life isn't over, it's just beginning (and yes, I'm saying that again and again in this chapter, in case you needed a reminder, as I did in those dark years). So let's begin with a new thought right this second!

Chapter 2

I'm a ~~Failure~~ Success

Two-point-five kids, a white picket fence and a Honda Odyssey in the driveway—that's the American dream, and the image of success. Everyone pictures married couples raising a family and then sitting on the front porch watching the grandkids. One of my first thoughts when I got divorced and realized that dream was gone, was *I'm a failure*.

Women tend to think that we have failed if our family gets split up and we have to uproot our kids. We feel like a failure if we lose our jobs or lose our husbands. *What did I do wrong?*

The answer is—nothing. Divorce is a life change, not a failure. It took me a long time to learn that lesson. I remember going to a barbecue at one of my friends' houses. She and her husband and kids seemed so bright and sunny and happy, and I sat there in my black outfit and mourned the death of my own life. Yeah, I was in a pretty dark place, I have to say.

Grieving the Memories

My mind would take me back to a family vacation and I could see the smiles on our children's faces as they beamed at their mother and father. They felt safe and secure, their world was predictable and complete. I remembered the two of us sitting on the edge of the bed when one of them was sick. I pictured cheering our kids on at their soccer games, clapping proudly at their piano recitals, and first days of school going forward, and saw a hole. I took joy in making homemade chicken pot pies with everyone's initials carved into the crust, eating warm chocolate chip cookies fresh out of the oven and pizza and movies every Friday night. Had I failed my children?

> Divorce is a life change, not a failure.

My son asked me one day after the divorce, "Mom, are we poor?"

"Why would you ask a question like that?" I asked.

"Because we don't even have cable anymore." In that moment, I realized how many things had changed and fallen by the wayside because of my dark days. I saw the impact on my children and that only reiterated my feelings of failure.

In fact, I felt so much like a failure that I kept almost everything to myself. My co-workers never knew I had family problems until almost a year after my divorce. I was ashamed and could not face my own reality. At times, I'd be enjoying my newly single life, but then I'd catch a glimpse of a married couple and the "Whys" would kick in. *Why did I get married? Why did I get divorced? Why wasn't I good enough? Why was I alone? Why didn't I do more for myself? Why hadn't I been more valuable and relevant in my life?* I kept thinking maybe I deserved what had happened to me. Self-doubt was eating me alive. It can do the same to you if you don't reverse that thinking.

Making the Transition

Those years between divorce and now were filled with transition. I went from being married, with the classic happily ever-after picture to single and struggling emotionally, to finally finding happiness. One of my first steps was to take down old photos in my home of my married life. I still had family pictures on my wall and mantles. I went through my jewelry and got rid of anniversary gifts regardless of value. My family and friends came over and helped repaint the interior and exterior of my home. I revamped my kid's bedrooms to their liking to include them in the transition. It was not an easy journey; it was a process. If you are struggling right now, don't be hard on yourself or think that your life is over or that you can never change. The impossible can be possible with time, patience, and action.

The first step is acceptance: This event happened, and whatever road you took to get there is a road that is in your rearview mirror. I struggled with feelings of failure because I had purposely chosen married life over college, emulating what I saw around me. How could I get that so wrong?

Healing wasn't possible until I faced my troubling thoughts. This is where the mindset makeover has its most power. I had to tell myself that I couldn't turn back the hands on the clock. My past life was a point in time that served a purpose.

Step One: Find the Purpose

That's a key point—***everything you go through serves a purpose***. By finding that purpose, you can begin to heal. For me, the good purpose that came out of my past was two beautiful children who love me unconditionally.

Step Two: Reframe and Reposition

The second step is reframing what happened. I didn't fail; I moved on to the next chapter in my life. See how that little tweak makes a huge difference in your thinking?

Step Three: Bury and Move On

Third, give yourself permission to grieve. I allowed myself to reminisce, but with tears of joy for the beautiful memories I had. Have you heard the term "bury the dead?" It was time for me to do away with any unpleasant flashbacks and bury them so that I could move forward. I would leave that feeling of failure behind and embark on a path of self-fulfillment. You too must move past the negative thinking.

> Write every negative thing you are feeling in a letter to yourself. Read it, shed tears if you need to, then tear it up into teeny, tiny pieces. Burn it, bury it, but do something that signifies you are done with those thoughts.

Focus on the New You

Starting life with a fresh perspective infused life into my mind, body and spirit. I moved forward from thinking I was a failure to seeking success, with one difference—I redefined my idea of success. To me, success wasn't about money or picket fences. It became about achieving milestones, self-development, self-care and making an impact within my circle and beyond.

I wanted to be a new person, and I wanted that person to be ageless. Not only on the outside—but on the inside. Ageless, to me, means you are flourishing and rejuvenating, both inside and out. Change has to start there first before the physical changes occur, or even work. Your mindset has to be right for everything else to fall into place. Later on we will address the exterior changes you can make, and how this completes the path to a new ageless you!

Find a New Purpose

I needed to break out and do something new that would give me a purpose point. I joined a direct sales company where I harnessed my skills of talking one-on-one to customers and shifted it into speaking in front of hundreds of people and leading a team of entrepreneurs. This is also where I discovered the science of anti-aging and methods ordinary people can use to recapture their youthfulness.

My purpose went back to my childhood. My mother had always instilled in us the value of taking care of our body and skin, and focusing on taking care of myself (and showing others how to do the same) seemed like coming full circle.

You too must find your purpose point, the thing that clicks for you and makes you feel good inside. What is it that you have always wanted to do? What are you good at? What is it that others see in you and routinely remind you of, saying that you are missing your calling? This is your purpose point. Within your purpose you will find your niche of happiness.

> **ONE THING TO DO TODAY**
>
> Find your purpose point. Make a list of five things that are meaningful to you. Working with children, gardening, reading, exercising, etc. How can you turn one of those things into an action that gives back and helps others?

Build Yourself Up

The power of positive thinking is extremely important in your self-development. Every time I saw a quote of empowerment, I saved it, printed it, and shared it. Success isn't all about you—it's about sharing that journey and the treasures you gain along the way with others. I would text my friends or post on social media positive messages and quotes about hope, coping, happiness, and thankfulness.

I took that a step further and started doing the same when speaking to others, even total strangers. My friends will tell you that I always find good things to say about people. That's because I look for the silver lining in every cloud.

As you are building yourself up by lifting others, watch what you fill those spaces inside yourself with. What we talk about, think about, and read about reveals what *we* are all about. Start to fill your mind with good things and happy thoughts. I tend to stay away from horrible stories, dark, gray, and depressing things (and wearing the color black!). I realized all that negativity wasn't good for my mind and detrimental to my success. In a later chapter we will discuss how you are what you eat—it's the same with your mind. You become what you consume with your brain. I cannot stress this enough: **the power of positive thinking is a master tool in life.**

Make a Difference

If you want to truly feel like a success—give back. I have found the most joy in hearing someone tell me, "Thank you for making my life better". This gratitude is so much better than money. Giving of yourself and your resources to enrich the lives of other people is very rewarding and will have benefits you never expected.

One time, I drove two hours to take a goodie basket to a friend who had been sick for a while. She was delighted when we showed up with a basket filled with natural, organic foods and products from a local health food store. This was better than a text message, email, card, or a quick "get better" on social media. I have done pet sitting for friends who travel, or offered to run errands for overwhelmed women in my circle. These are little things that make the biggest difference for others, and in doing that, you will find a huge difference in you, too.

Always Be Sincere

No matter what you do, always be real with your intentions. Everything that I have done for others is genuine and comes straight from my heart. If you complete an act of kindness, don't look for the kudos. The value of your gift is then negated, and people will see through that. No one likes to be reminded of something that you did for them because it fills them with guilt and makes them wish you had never done it.

My acts of kindness and giving started with my friends, meaning the people that I already shared a natural bond of love. Then I looked for worthy organizations to donate my time and resources to. There are plenty of ways to become involved to help others, but no matter what, it cannot be about financial gain or public attention.

In direct sales we have a phrase: ***Your Why Must Make You Cry***. If your why and your purpose fills your heart, then you are doing the right thing. Your reason for doing these things will be genuine and show in everything you do and say.

My divorce didn't mean my life was over; it was just beginning. To ignite that restart I had to shift from thinking failure to realizing success was found in doing and giving. That was the switch in my mind that moved me from a zero to a hero to myself. It didn't happen overnight and I had to take baby steps, easing into some of these long-term changes. You can do it too. Start by developing ageless thoughts and intentions. I want you to become open to new ideas and consider new interests (more on that in another chapter). Doing so will mean coming out of your comfort zone, but it's going to be okay, I promise. I did it and so can you!

The Mirror Moment

Ask yourself: **"Do I feel like I am a failure in life?"**

If so, then it's time to make a change. Start by reframing your thinking and crossing out the thinking that leads to negativity about yourself. Change the words you think and speak and you will start redirecting your mind down that road to success.

Now, turn the page to find out how your purpose can impact your self-worth!

Chapter 3

I Have ~~No Worth~~ So Much Worth

My transformation, as I mentioned, wasn't overnight. I went to see a therapist because I felt worthless. This was a new experience for me and I didn't know what to expect. Walking into her office I noticed a box of tissues on the table and I wondered why it was there. Halfway through my first session I was reaching for the tissue to wipe away tears. I had not come to terms with the fact that I needed to regain my inner self-worth back to a positive state of mind. After several sessions I learned how powerful the mind is over the body. As I slowly replaced each black piece of clothing in my closet, so too did I start replacing the negative thoughts in my head. Once your mind makeover begins, the other parts—self and body—fall into place, which is why they are ordered that way in this book. We're sort of doing this journey together, as if I was your best friend and holding your hand as you make one change after another.

Doing this alone is hard. For a while I kept it a secret that I had sought the help of a therapist. As I began to listen to other people who had gone through a break up and had also seen a therapist, I realized there is no shame in talking to a third party, someone not connected to your life, who simply listens and reaffirms you into a positive mindset. Changing yourself and your thinking isn't a cake walk for anyone. So many famous people on the outside seem to have it all, but underneath all the fame and glitter and designer labels, many of them are suffering from a lack of inner self worth, sometimes to the point of self-destruction (think of Britany Spears, for example). Even for ordinary people like you and me, this path of self-destructiveness tries to get the best of you, and you have to fight, as I did, to hold onto yourself. Step by step, my life was coming together but I still had a few more hurdles to overcome.

Where is My Real Value?

My divorce left my self-esteem shattered. There were times in those years when I got off a team call or finished up some leadership training and doubted myself and my value. I questioned whether the people I worked with saw real value in me as person. My career was centered on trading time for money, essentially, I give you eight hours and you give me a check. I struggled, however, with whether what I was providing was worth the monetary gain.

> As I slowly replaced each black piece of clothing in my closet, so too did I start replacing the negative thoughts in my head.

For many of us, our careers define us. Think about it—when someone is quoted in the news or on television, they're defined by three things: their name, their age, and their job. A job gives us a sense of self-worth and contribution toward something. That's hard to find if you are robotically performing daily functions in your workplace. I had become almost a robot in my job, and that contributed to my struggle with my sense of worth, and meaning. I wasn't looking for recognition, but rather the feelings that come from acts of goodwill.

If you are struggling with those same feelings of self-doubt, questioning your value and worth, I want to tell you that you are not alone. That you can and will be able to turn those thoughts around (without having to change jobs, unless you want to!). Those new feelings come from within, and…here's the key: **your thoughts on your value are not contingent on whether you are making widgets or saving the environment in your daily job.**

Fake it Until You Make It

There's a reason that's a popular phrase—because it's true. Sometimes, you have to pretend you have self-worth before it's actually instilled inside you. Even when my own inner beliefs were shaky, I started acting like I had value in the workplace, and projecting an image of value. I knew that I wanted to expand my professional and community circles, so that I could find opportunities to give back.

I started small, with new business cards. I wanted my business cards to convey not just what I do, but also that I am an activist with a love for the heart of our community. Why business cards? Because the first step in expanding your connections is showing up prepared, with business cards.

However, if you have a business card, it doesn't work if the person handing it out is as cold as ice. You have to be *warmly* professional. What do I mean by warmly? Your aura should be approachable, welcoming and professional.

If the idea of moving out of your circle scares you, practice saying a greeting in the mirror, with a friend, or record a video of yourself on your cell phone. Don't criticize your performance— celebrate the things you do well, and build on those.

Ditching the Black

If you meet me in person today, you'll see color everywhere. Eight years ago, I wore black from head to toe—tops, pants, skirts, sun dress, shorts, bathing suits, cover ups, etc. The dress code for my new future, goals, and purpose, was not black. Even though I had some cute black dresses and outfits, I didn't want to wake up every day and feel like I was attending a funeral. I was in a vibrant community, filled with energetic people and I wanted to reflect that energy.

Black told a story for me for a long time, but it was time to make a change. In a later chapter, we will talk about style and fashion and how color can make an impact. For now, I'm focusing on how you could be sabotaging your own mindset by dressing in a manner that is directly opposite from your message and goals.

Growing with Humility

The more I did for others, the more I *wanted* to do for others. I used vacation PTO hours from work to attend community networking and charity events. Thankfully, my employer supported my activities and happily granted me time off when I requested it. The more I gave back, the more I gained trust among my community and the greater sense of self-worth I developed. By now, people from all walks of life began to reach out to me for guidance, coaching, support and as a person of action. My adult children started seeing me as more than just Mom—they saw me as a connector for goodwill.

If you can give of your resources to your community, you will feel this same new sense of self. I'm not talking about just money. You can give time, skills, or things. You can do volunteer work, provide marketing for nonprofits, or simply support an event by donating in kind.

A close friend of mine asked for help in developing her business market. I said no to being on the payroll, but yes to helping where I could. I didn't have a lot of free time but I wanted to make time for what was important, and she was important to me. I'm not saying that you are not entitled to compensation for products, goods, and services that you provide. Don't be that person who only does things when you are being paid. You are building something much bigger than a paycheck here. Yes, the old saying is that money doesn't grow on trees—but neither does self-worth.

Look for causes that matter to you and touch your heart, whether it be organizations that help single parents, battered women, foster children, rescue animals, or environmental causes. At the end of the day, you will likely be tired, but your heart will be full and your memories overflowing.

Your Value is Unlimited

"Sabrina, name your number; I will give you anything you want." I still remember hearing those words from the owner of a company where I was interviewing for a position to help grow their business. I sat there, and couldn't come up with a number. I didn't know my own value and couldn't name my salary. What was I worth in terms of dollars?

I was not prepared to make a complete career change and move into fulltime work for another firm. Even a greater salary offer would not give me the fulfillment that I was looking for. Working this part-time gig opened up so many doors for me in the professional community and among my peers. My friends began to see me as a connector and recommended me to other professionals. My professional and community circle broadened and I was in demand. While I enjoyed the marketing position it also made me realize my value financially and professionally. I left that position and started carving my own path into my own business. We will talk more about that in the next chapter.

Be Wary of Overcommitting

It's easy to get super excited about the new opportunities and challenges in your life. The more I volunteered and expanded my network, the more my calendar filled up. I felt bad turning down event invites and lunches. Then I realized that this was all part of valuing my worth.

> **ONE THING TO DO TODAY**
>
> Several times throughout the day, I want you to say to yourself: "I do have self-worth." It may seem silly but this affirmation can add years back into your life by making you feel useful, needed, and wanted.

My time is worth something to others—and it is also worth something to me. Read that over again, if you're one of those women who gives and gives and gives. Who has trouble saying no, or who feels guilty when she skips out on an event. *Your time is worth something to yourself.*

Part of knowing your self-worth is knowing when you need self-care. A day to recharge, an afternoon to put your feet up, or an evening doing something fun that you love. Repeating to yourself that your time is worth something to yourself can help you to pull back when you are tempted to overcommit.

Having an Ageless Mindset

One of the more powerful (and goal-cementing) things I did was to sit down at my computer and spend hours writing down my mission, my values, and my vision (MVV) statement for myself. As I found my purpose, I wanted to be sure that every decision I made followed that path. I knew I wanted to go forth with spreading the word about being ageless, but to do that, I had to start with an ageless mind.

What is an ageless mind? One that realizes you can live a timeless life right now. Don't wait to be thinner or younger or richer. **Wake up! Get up! Stand up! It's time to reactivate and cultivate the new you!** Download my ageless mindset worksheet from my website.

Loving that New Kid on the Block

By now all of my friends, family, and co-workers had started noticing the changes in my thinking and how I carried myself (not to mention the more colorful wardrobe!). The Mindset Makeover had taken over and was shifting my life into a better place more each day. Over a period of time, I was able to move past a divorce and get out of the mental dungeon. The content of my conversations was redirected from the negative *poor me* to a positive, *how can I help you*?

I had to learn to love the person that I saw in the mirror each day. I stopped feeling sorry for that woman and embraced the good things about this new me. You can do that too.

If you're sitting there saying, *I don't have good things to embrace*, let me tell you that you couldn't be more wrong. We *all* have value. We all have something to give to the world. And we all have value to ourselves. Go back to the MVV statement. Those are the bedrocks from which you can build this new thinking and way of being. Put it where you can see it every day—on the fridge, on your mirror, on the car dashboard. Surround yourself with the people who believe in you, support you and build you into your best self. You may need to seek out new friends and connections, but that's okay. It's all about helping you thrive and grow as a person. If you feel suffocated, unheard, or discarded by anyone in your life—cut them out and move on. Do not allow *anyone* to make you feel like less of a person. It's not just your time that is worth something to you—it is your entire being that is worth more than any number can count.

If you only take one thing from this chapter (or from this entire book), I hope it is this: Love YOU and others will too.

Now turn the page to find out how your new Mindset Makeover is a prelude to the next levels of an ageless and better you!

The Mirror Moment

"Do I feel that I have no worth?"

If your answer is *yes,* then it's time to make a change. Start by reframing your thinking and crossing out the thinking that leads to negativity about yourself. Stop finding fault when you look in the mirror. Instead of criticizing yourself, *value* yourself. Tell yourself that you are not worthless and that you are worth more than the finest gold.

Part Two

SELF MAKEOVER

Chapter 4

I Like ~~Being Alone~~ Building Connections

In those first few weeks after my divorce, all I wanted to do was stay inside my house, close the drapes and not see another human being. I went to work, but had little interest in doing anything else. If not for the kids, I probably would have gone back to bed as soon as I got home. I was in mourning for a dream, and embarrassed by what had happened, and still licking my wounds. Like many divorced people, I told myself I was better off alone.

That's not true. It's a lie we tell ourselves that creates a vicious cycle of solitude, depression, more solitude and more depression. We stay in the dark, literally and figuratively, and can't see the bright world waiting outside those closed blinds.

The Homebody

When I was younger, I was always surrounded by a network of people. I had friends and coworkers, and I socialized often. Then I got married and had two kids, and like many women, my world narrowed into just us four. I had gotten socially lazy and wasn't making friends or going out.

For many of us, as we get older we become "homebodies" and "couch potatoes," creating a self-fulfilling prophecy. We can become prisoners in our own homes and not realize it. Think that hasn't happened to you? Then ask yourself this: Are you home by 6pm, eating dinner alone by 7 pm, watching your favorite show at 8pm and then in bed by 9:30 pm? Are you texting friends instead of seeing them in person? Spending your weekends buying groceries and cleaning? Avoiding girls' night or neighborhood barbecues? How many people are you actively interacting with during the day? The week?

I had become a homebody/couch potato, or whatever you want to call it. My world had become tiny and I knew that improving my self-worth started with expanding my circle. I was determined that I was going to get back to interacting with people as a means to regain vitality and self-relevance.

Start with the Inner Circle

When you begin building connections, it's easier to start from the inside and widen out. By that I mean starting with the people you are already connected to (and may have not talked to in a while). I started with my friends, and through association, they helped me bridge out to meet other people.

The first thing I did was say yes to a dinner invitation from a longtime friend. Her dinner parties were legendary—as few as four or as many as thirty people at a time. My mission that evening was to mingle, converse, and get contact information. Establishing a contact list in my phone, complete with names and cell numbers, gave me the tools to broaden my warm circle (remember how I talked about being warmly professional in Chapter Three? A warm circle is one comprised of people you are already friendly with, e.g., warm).

When you begin expanding your own warm circle, don't get nervous about asking for contact and/or social media information. We live in a world of technology; this is how people connect now. I normally add a note in my phone as to where I met that person and what they do. Some people add a photo with every contact so that the person's picture appears when they call. That's a little more personal, so be sure to ask permission from your new contact to do that. I usually only ask to add a photo if we have talked for a while and it seems that we have a good connection.

Coming Out as You

After about ten months of broadening my warm circle and developing friends through friends, it was time for me to come out and embrace my self-makeover. I decided I was going to do this in style! After all, I had a new me I wanted to celebrate and lots of new friends I wanted to appreciate, so I threw myself a sophisticated after-five party at my house, for men and women. This was a first for me as I had never entertained multiple guests at home by myself. I was nervous, but ready.

Don't wait until you lose ten pounds or you get your hair colored or you have a new job to celebrate and add life back into your life. Aren't you ready to feel worthy, valuable, and good? I was, and that was worth ordering colorful tablecloths, pretty dinnerware, velvety chair covers, and matching sashes. I made all the food from scratch, from appetizers to dessert. I displayed the food on fine serving platters trimmed in silver. It was elegant and beautiful—and it was the most fun I had had in years. I felt ageless, and alive. You know I didn't wear black, either! I chose a gorgeous royal blue dinner party dress that made me feel classy and attractive again. I was celebrating me, and I was going to contribute everything I could to that party.

Protect the Pack

I had a wider and great new community of comrades, but I also had my "pack," my group of go-to girls who were my closest friends. If you have friends like this, protect those friendships. They are vital for support and cheering. My pack and I organized weekend getaways within a day's travel, planned some fun girls' nights out with dinner, wine, and good conversation. My pack has about ten women in it, and they're always game for anything. Our outings included: formal events, taking dance lessons, barbeques at rotating homes, beach time, game night, bonfires, talent events, and karaoke. All fun experiences that took us out of our comfort zones. It wasn't so scary to do those things with close friends.

If you don't already have a pack, start to build one. My core group of friends was made possible from a seedling of one friend that grew into a group, all because I made the effort to mix with people. You can do the same. Ask a good friend to co-host a dinner party or plan a night out with others and start to build a new circle. Make it simple and relaxed, and in a location that allows for conversation. A loud band will overpower any new friendships you are trying to make.

Over time, my second husband became part of the pack (more on him later). It was great because we hung out in the same circle and had a lot of similar interests. I want you to know and believe that a lot of wonderful things can happen when you make a firm resolve to connect with people.

Networking for Tomorrow

Think about your future. Where do you want to be in the next five to ten years? What will you need to do to get there? If you're having trouble figuring out this answer, go back to the purpose you named in an earlier chapter. Your purpose, remember, is your touchstone for everything going forward.

I had career plans, and knew how to get from A to B in my career, but when it came to my personal life, I floundered for a while. I knew that I wanted to find roots and keep busy with people and projects that had meaning. That meant it was time for me to build value in the business community beyond employment. Having a job takes care of the bills, but having a side gig (side hustle) or hobby is self-actualization. Whatever this is, should be an innate thing that feels completely natural to you to do, and that brings you pleasure (and sometimes income; money should not be the primary goal).

How do you get there? By networking. Today, there is no shortage of networking groups that meet anywhere, anytime, in person or online. Find a group that matches your values and whose mission and visions you can embrace. Be sure to check out the groups a couple times before committing with a membership fee. Beware of the party groups that meet during happy hour. This is nothing more than people transitioning from work to home with a pit stop in between, and an excuse to have wine. It doesn't have purpose (see the recurring theme?).

Look for groups that fit your personality, yet encourage you to stretch your wings a little. If you're naturally timid and not a mingler, try to find a group that isn't high-pressure on public speaking. Remember, the goal is to build your community and essentially, your future world.

In my early years of networking I burned up the road traveling from one group to the other, meeting people, shaking hands, and collecting business cards. That was fun for a while and I did meet some interesting people. But unlike the circle of friends I had created, there were no relationships beyond the meetings I attended. After a year of wear and tear on me and my car, I decided to start my own women's networking organization that focused on building relationships, gaining business exposure, and giving back to the community. More information on my Tampa Bay group is at the back of this book, if you want to come by and check out a meeting!

Empower Yourself

For most of my life, I worked in corporations in a predominately male environment. Because I was one of a handful of women, I learned how to stand on my own two feet and developed leadership skills along the way. All those lessons I was unwittingly learning later helped me develop my women's empowerment and networking organization.

I started with one member—me and then I hand-picked women business owners I knew from other groups and asked them if they wanted to meet regularly to grow and expand their networks. When I started W.E.E., Women's Entrepreneurial Empowerment, I had four women, but it soon grew as word spread and grew as members brought other members to meetings. Suddenly, my life had more purpose because I was helping to enrich the lives and paths of others. Little did I know just how life-changing this group would prove to be for me.

Why would I do all this? Because I firmly believe *you cannot grow unless you help others grow.* Your field will multiply in size if you help others plant. That's what happened with W.E.E.. We started expanding and bringing in speakers (which pushed me beyond my comfort zone because I had to ask professionals in our community to present at our meetings). I presented myself as a professional with experience with linking people together, and actually developed a wait list for speakers. It worked so well, because I had learned the art of expanding my network in my warm circle of friends. That old saying, bloom where you are planted, can be applied here— take the area you are already in and expand and grow. Then pass on that growth to others. If you don't want to start your own group, attach your network to an organization with a purpose and donate your resources wherever possible.

Focus on Giving

Even as my life got busier and bigger, I kept making charity a big part of my life. W.E.E. had a charitable arm, and we chose to support Dress for Success Tampa Bay, a nonprofit organization focused on supporting women in the community by suiting them in business attire for employment. Our first year, W.E.E. hosted a clothing drive that resulted in over three hundred pieces of clothing and accessories being donated. The media picked up on our cause and publicized it, too, which meant I was speaking on camera.

Here I am only a year after recovering from depression, loneliness, and isolation. I was amazed as I sat in front of TV cameras and felt like I was in my prime, with this ageless attitude leading to open doors. Think back to how dark it got for me—literally dark in the closed blinds and head-to-toe black. If I can do this, you can do it, believe me.

The Leader Within

As the interviews piled up, my voice grew. It was such a surprising thing, because after my divorce, I felt like I had no voice. So many women feel that way, too. As if they're speaking but people aren't listening. Maybe you stay quiet because you don't believe that you have anything of value to add.

It took time, but my life gradually unfolded with great joy, perspective, and purpose. I came from humble beginnings on this journey of self-worth, and I did it one step at a time. It's not necessary to take leadership classes or undergo special training to learn how to network and grow. Most of my skills have come from simply doing it—interacting with people, reading about inspirational people, and embracing the real me.

The words others speak to you and that you speak to yourself have power. One of my guest speakers, a judge, said to me, "Sabrina, you are a leader." Wow, just hearing her say that empowered me and planted a seed in my head. "I am a leader," I thought to myself. Those words had never crossed my mind before, and hearing them rewrote the tape in my mind. From that moment forward, I realized that I could impact the lives of others in a positive way.

> **ONE THING TO DO TODAY**
>
> Make one new connection today. Just one. Find someone with common interests and goals at work, at the gym, at your favorite restaurant, or on your morning walk. Make this new connection a meaningful one.

Sometimes we just need someone else to speak it about us or write it about us, and then we become it. It's mental conditioning. I learned leadership skills at work, but that was in a controlled environment. This type of leadership was one of influencing and impacting others, both friends and perfect strangers, and encouraging them to take some type of action.

If you've never heard it before, let me say it to you now: **You, too, are a leader.** You may lead in a different way or different discipline, but you have power that can be used to empower others.

Networking, leading, speaking, engaging—these are just more ways of adding life back into life. The ageless journey is one of creating opportunity, regardless of your biological number.

Go back to the beginning of this chapter and re-read the statement makeover: My life is not over – It's just beginning. By that same token: **I am ~~too old~~ ready to start something new.**

Now, turn the page to find out how to thrive and live agelessly within your new circle!

The Mirror Moment

"Have I allowed myself to become a homebody or a couch potato?"

If you have, then it's time to make a change. Start by reframing your thinking and crossing out the thoughts that lead to a lack of mental energy and an unwillingness to engage with other people. Get out there, and expand your warm circle. Surround yourself with people who help you grow so you can do the same to the next woman who needs a reminder that she is amazing.

Chapter 5

~~I'm Afraid~~ I'm Taking Chances

I stared at the family room wall, hesitant to cover the beige paint. For years, I'd lived in those safe lanes of beige and white in my décor. One of my friends had encouraged me to think outside the box and try a new look. Burgundy.

Such a bold, bright color was a huge step for me. I stood there, thinking about all the times I'd been afraid to take a chance, afraid to be different, afraid to be myself. No more. By the end of that weekend, I had a burgundy accent wall, and another wall in a soft butternut squash. If I ever decided to sell my house, it would be an easy transition back to neutral colors. In the meantime, I intended to fill my home and life with things and colors that brought joy to me and my kids. When I was done painting, I went shopping and picked out new furnishings that reflected this bold new direction.

Broaden Your Horizons

That trip to Hawaii was the start of many more trips, for pleasure, and also for work. I used to be so afraid to travel alone, but now I was booking flights, staying in hotels, and gaining information. I took three or four trips a year for my network marketing organization. All that travel represented big growth moments because I had to independently fund and make all of my travel and lodging arrangements.

I was scared at first, but soon learned how to navigate the different options and sites. On every trip, I had so much fun and met so many new people, but most of all, I came away energized and ready to apply what I learned. Some people I have met think it's a waste to spend that kind of time and money on motivational enlightenment experiences. To me, investing in myself is important. I'd spend easily that much on a three-day trip to a theme park or a season of sporting events.

If you're hesitating, look at it as investment in *yourself*. These kinds of experiences can build up your mind and character, expand your network, and enhance your speaking skills. Find what works for you, and go for whatever enrichment you need to be the best self you can be. I find that I learn better at live events and via audio/video training. You might prefer printed books, and classroom-style learning. Whichever you choose, take the time and energy to invest in your most precious resource—yourself.

Step out of Your Comfort Zone

Trips and seminars were one thing, but I decided to take the concept of trying new things a little further. I signed up for a scuba diving lesson, held in a swimming pool. I was nervous and scared, and even more so when I strapped on the diving helmet. It seemed too close, too hard to breathe, but still I got into the pool and tried. I wasn't going to say no, just because this was a new experience. The helmet didn't work well for me, so I opted for a regular face mask and oxygen tank, and that worked perfectly. I stood on the bottom of the pool, in a completely new world, and so very proud of myself for moving out of my safe space. Before, I never would have tried something like this. But I was a new me, and this new woman wanted to experience all that life had to offer.

For you, stepping out of your comfort zone could be something as simple as striking up a conversation with a stranger on an airplane. I've done that dozens of times, and many of the people I have met remain in my network of friends today. The self-development workshops and other things that I did gave me the confidence to strike up a conversation with a perfect stranger, no matter where I was. On one trip when I was looking for a good place to eat, I stopped two women and asked their opinion. We struck up a conversation and they invited me to their corporate lunch the next day. Thirty other people were at that event, a great networking opportunity for me. More than that, though, I made friends. We took pictures, laughed hysterically and at the same time built more connections. That once-depressed woman was stepping out with a fresh self-makeover, and I couldn't be more excited.

> **ONE THING TO DO TODAY**
>
> Start a mental bucket list. The first thing on the list should be an out-of-the-box action item.
>
> Now write it down too. Don't just think it…ink it. Make this list something that you can take pride and joy in. Fill it with things that are meaningful to you.
>
> Don't leave that list on the fridge to gather dust. Start checking things off!

Spread the Good Words

Just as I needed to hear good things about myself, other women and men need that confidence boost as well. When you talk to a stranger, or a new connection, do so with a friendly, complimentary tone. When I was on a trip, the hotel I was at was busy and hectic, but the two front desk employees gave expedient service with a smile. I struck up a conversation and complimented them. They were millennials, and so young, we shouldn't have had anything in common, but we did. Everyone likes to hear they look good, they did a good job, or they're a good person. The hotel employees were so thankful, they gave me full access to the VIP room and free breakfast for three days. I didn't say any of those things with the intent of receiving something in return, and never would. Making people feel good has a boomerang effect, but it requires action.

Make Scary Career Steps

My momentum grew, which fueled me to start my own pre-retirement business to supplement my income for those future days I'd be spending on the beach without a care in the world. This was a big step. It's one thing to join a company but yet another to grow one from the ground up. It's all about belief and commitment, and tending that business garden every day with the right tools. I secured a business strategist, a brand developer, a social media guru, and a photographer. I developed my mission, vision and value statements, learned how to develop a website, and then I stepped out in faith.

Everything about that business, from the logo to the T-shirts, was about reflecting a life infused with vibrancy and rich colors. All of this was a new experience for me, in terms of having complete accountability, ownership, and financial commitment. It was scary, but I did it, and asked for help when I needed it. You can do the same.

One place where I stumbled in stepping out of my comfort zone was getting professional photos done. A part of me was still that woman who wore black for three years. On shoot day, I brought in a professional hairstylist and makeup artist. I hadn't worn mascara, eyeliner, and eye shadow since I was a teenager. When I looked in the mirror, I barely recognized myself.

My nerves and discomfort showed in the pictures. I was stiff as a board while trying to pose and smile for the camera. The photographer kept reminding me to breathe. I closed my eyes, drew in a breath, and told myself it would be okay. When I saw the proofs later, I saw a new, more vibrant woman than I used to be.

The Ageless Attitude

In those photos, I was ageless. I'm not talking about the number on my driver's license; I'm talking about an attitude. Agelessness is a mind, body, and spirit elixir. It's a shift in attitude and in self-care. Before I embraced agelessness, all I had in front of me was working forty years of my life to sock away forty percent of my pay, and then live off that for another twenty years. The word retirement brought to mind images of elderly, sedentary people engaged in weekly early-bird restaurant hopping. I didn't want that for myself. I want to drive my car, dress up, go places, and create memories, no matter what age I am.

The Ageless Techniques and Philosophy

Embracing agelessness pulled me out of the woods and made me whole again. It can do the same for you. Allow me to introduce you to Ageless Techniques. They can change your life.

- The basic tenet of Agelessness is: "Think Young – Live Younger"
- It's a lifestyle that includes: mindset, body care, diet, fitness, skin care, hair care, dress, grooming, and recreation

- Body care that includes natural, plant-based approaches to disrupting the aging cycle and regain your energy and vitality

- Designed for men and women over forty who want to live their best life *now*

- Focused on regaining mental vigor, natural wellness, anti-aging, and senior social lifestyle development

- All under the umbrella of one mission statement: *Ageless Techniques is bringing exhilaration to life, the mind, body, decorum and beauty while tapping into new technologies in natural wellness.*

For more information, check out our Webinar Series on Wellness, Fitness, and Dancing.

Never Stop Trying New Things

Muhammad Ali once said, "You are as old as you think you are." I keep this quote in my phone to remind myself not to regress into thinking that I am too old for anything. You, too, must adapt a firm resolve to not box yourself into a negative, non-productive mindset. When my seven-year-old granddaughter challenged me to a sprint race, I hesitated for a second, then said yes. Our granddaughter was so excited to try to beat Grandma in front of the neighborhood kids. My husband and our neighbors cheered us, right to the finish line. It didn't matter if I won. What matters is enjoying life and being active. Ageless is living and playing alongside your adult children and grandchildren, and never saying no to a fun new opportunity. (And if you really want to know who won, check out the video of the race in our Fitness Webinar).

Now, turn the page to find out why ageless is the *antidote* to boring!

The Mirror Moment

Ask yourself: "Am I living my life inside the box?"

If you answered *Yes* to that statement, then it's time to get out of the box! Start by reframing your thinking and crossing out any thoughts that have kept you literally boxed inside your world and your comfort zone. There is life outside there, and so many opportunities awaiting you.

Don't be afraid to take that first step to freedom. Look at your list, and pick one thing you've wanted to do for a long time but held yourself back. Do your research, then take a deep breath—

And try. You might be surprised how wonderful you feel when you stop worrying about staying in your lane.

Chapter 6

I Like ~~Predictability~~ Disrupting the Routine

Throw your talk in the fire or put some fire in your talk! When I was a teacher's assistant in a Dale Carnegie course, I heard that phrase many times. I had taken several courses and decided to come back as a volunteer to help others in their personal growth. Despite taking the courses, I still got very nervous when I had to deliver an unrehearsed speech. I liked the predictability of a speech with notes, one that I had memorized and knew wouldn't go off course. I was always worried about sounding like an idiot, and having a rehearsed, planned speech kept me from making mistakes in front of others.

One day, it was my turn to stand in front of thirty people and deliver a five-minute presentation on fear. As I returned to my chair the master instructor thanked me for my prepared speech. Then he said, "Now Sabrina is going to return to the stage and show us the right way to handle fear with an impromptu speech on the topic." I panicked for a second, but did as he said and climbed back onto the stage. I did it—improvised for the first in my life and even better, the class loved it. My speech was a bit boring and not that inspiring, but the class was enthusiastic about me rising to meet the challenge instead of resorting to what I knew, to my comfort zone.

Turn Off the Autopilot

Have you ever driven yourself home and wondered how you got there? You don't remember the turns or the red lights, and yet here you are, in your own driveway. That's kind of scary in one sense, yet shows us how powerful the mind is in another. You operated on autopilot, taking the same route as always. What about shopping in the grocery store? Do you find yourself putting the same items in your basket each week? You don't even look at the price or think about changing up the menu. Your hand automatically reaches for that one item and your mind tunes out all the other surrounding brands and choices.

Autopilot causes you to miss out on taking a chance. You could be trying something new, better tasting, or more effective. By making the same choices again and again, you're not stepping out of that lane you always travel. Sometimes that autopilot keeps you from thinking for yourself, too.

A funny story—one time after my divorce I decided to try a new recipe that called for lemon zest. I scoured the grocery stores around town, looking for it. No lemon zest anywhere. And why was that? All you bakers reading this know it's not something you buy; you make it by grating lemon rinds. I was so locked inside my mental routine that I was totally unaware of something so basic. In the end, I figured it out, and my lemon tart recipe turned out well, thank goodness.

If you find yourself operating on autopilot for everything from your commute to your dinner menu, change it up this week. Take a different route to work, make a new dish this week. Taking one step out of your routine leads to another and another, creating a whole new way of thinking and a whole new life!

Take a Minute to Experience the World

Most of us go through our days, totally unaware of our surroundings. We're focused on the destination, not the journey. Stop and smell the roses! When you do, you'll find various scents, smells, and varieties. You'll find a world of color and experiences that you have been missing. And while we're on the subject, when was the last time you purchased a rose for yourself? Why wait on someone else to give you something so delicate and beautiful? Self-care is about doing and experiencing the things that bring you joy.

Part of stopping to notice the world around you is engaging with that world, too. We live our lives at a fast pace, zipping through drive-throughs for food, using drive-up teller banking, and express lane self-checkout. What happened to personally interacting with people? We get so used to this distant interaction that we forget there are people on the other side of the machines.

I make it a point to break the routine and meet my bankers and speak with restaurant managers. I engage with everyone from the busboy to the supermarket cashier, and try to express gratitude for good food and good service at every opportunity. I do this to engage with my world, and to truly see the people within it.

Show Appreciation to Others

Thanking people, sometimes with a small gift or gratuity, is another way to disrupt that automaton routine. Have you ever thought about gifting your favorite manager, waiter or waitress? Appreciation is ageless and timeless. You are never too old or too young to give and receive thanks.

You don't have to give money—you can give time or graciousness. Hold the door for another person, give up your seat to someone who needs it more, offer to help a neighbor. When you do these things, you will feel great and the other people will too. It took going through a divorce and learning to focus less on me and more on others, to finally embrace growth and the ageless mindset of being happy by making others happy.

Pay Attention to Routines—and Break Them

How many times do you walk into your favorite restaurant week after week and before you open your mouth to order, the kitchen is already working on your food? You never make a change to your order, and the staff knows it. I used to have a favorite soup and salad place that I visited daily for lunch. Every day, I ordered the same crab soup. The waitress put in the order as soon as I walked in the door, and I had the exact change for the order. One day the price was thirty cents higher and that change derailed my mind. While I had been plodding along with the same routine, the restaurant had been changing (and raising their prices to reflect that change).

That moment was a wake-up call. I started trying new places for lunch and sometimes bringing my lunch from home. I got so energized by the idea of varying my predictable routine that I started doing weekend meal prep for breakfast and lunch for the week.

That's not to say that all routines have to be disrupted. Keeping sacred things sacred does not equate to boring and predictable. For example, Friday night is date night for my husband and I. We maintained this tradition during our courtship and to this day as man and wife. Every Friday night, we dress up and go out to dinner, to see a movie, or on an adventure just like teenagers. When we do this, we feel ageless and carefree. From time to time, if something really critical comes up, we have shifted that date to a weekend day, but we always have a date night. By setting that time aside for each other we keep our bond strong. We've included my daughter and granddaughter on date nights, and made sure that our evenings leave us with lasting memories.

Keep Track of What's Most Important

So often, we end up on a hamster wheel of wake up, go to work, come home, cook dinner, clean up, go to bed, repeat, repeat, repeat. We're afraid of shaking things up because we fear disrupting everything. Things change—be prepared for that by embracing the need to change yourself.

I had to learn balance as I came into my own. A new husband, founding W.E.E. (Women's Entrepreneurial Empowerment), and fueling up my online Ageless Techniques business required more time resources and for a while, I felt pulled in dozens of directions. I sat down one day and decided on my non-negotiables—the things that I would maintain, no matter what. These may seem silly but they were important, and kept me engaged with the most important people in my life.

> **ONE THING TO DO TODAY**
>
> Try any of these things today:
> - Taste a new food
> - Try a new recipe
> - Tip someone for good service
> - Give a gift to someone who isn't expecting it
> - Perform an act of loving kindness for another, for no reason.

1. Ongoing game of Words with Friends with my mom
2. Spending time with my husband
3. Making daily time for spiritual worship
4. Touching base with important friends daily
5. Dedicating one night a week to my newest endeavors

I have developed a schedule, but not a routine, for these meaningful things in my life. There is a difference between the two. To me, a routine is a perfunctory, mechanical, or habitual task that is absent of feelings or emotions. It's like reading a speech that is so well prepared, you bore yourself speaking it. On the other hand, a schedule is a reservation of time for something important, an event or person that is deserving of your respect and commitment. How do you know if what you are doing is a routine or a schedule? Start by understanding what you are doing and why you are doing it. That will help you determine that event's value and where it falls in your life.

Don't Be Afraid to Go Off the Grid

By turning off all electronics and completely unplugging, you can disrupt your routine—and get a much-needed recharge. I had always wanted to stay in a hotel directly on the beach, but when I had vacation time, none of my friends were available. I booked a room at the Resort in Longboat Key, with a view of the white sand and aqua blue water. It felt a little odd when I checked in alone. I had no one to talk to, no one to go to the beach or have dinner with, but that was also what I needed. The meditation time was good for me and it helped me get on track with a few things.

Do not overlook the need to disconnect when life gets hectic. Maybe a trip alone is not possible for you, but you can have a stay-cation in your own residence. Turn your phone off and let everything go to voicemail for a day or two. You will be amazed at how energized you feel at the end of your self-cation. You'll also realize that you haven't missed much by staying off social media and avoiding the news. Peace of mind promotes a positive, healthy outlook in life. The positivity gives you the courage to continue disrupting your routine and stepping out of your comfort zone. In the end, you will feel refreshingly ageless!

Give When There is No Reason to Give

With the people we love, we often get into a routine—gifts for weddings, anniversaries, graduations, and new baby births. I talk to my mother long distance every day and my siblings almost as often. The communication is a delightful gift for me and my mother. I call her at different times of the day, never a set time or topic to discuss, which keeps it a pleasant surprise for both of us.

I decided to take this a step further after my mother and sister remarked on a strand of pearls I had bought for myself. I thought there was no sense in waiting for a specific day to show them how much I treasured them. That week, I bought them each a necklace and mailed them, along with a card expressing my love and appreciation. They were surprised and happy to receive this unexpected gift. I've done the same with dresses they like, or things I see that make me think of them. They do the same for me, for no other reason than love. Look for ways to show your love for your family and friends with little

---

DON'T BE PREDICTABLY DULL

You should be a breath of fresh air when people meet you, interact with you or embrace you in their circle. Your smile should be contagious and the content of your conversations should be uniquely interesting. Boring, routine and predictable is no fun, not for you and not for those in your circle.

Have fun disrupting your own routine by exploring new options in everything that you do. Here are some ideas:

Enhance others' lives with words of inspiration

Spontaneously invite a few friends over for coffee, cards, or light snacks

Accept an invitation you would usually decline

Share something fun or unique with a loved one

Try to introduce one new topic of conversation in your daily interactions

acts of kindness that are not related to special occasions or annual celebrations.

Being ageless is about not being predictable and embracing all the variety that life offers you. Every day, take one step out of your routine, and soon you'll find yourself on a new, exciting path that brings more life to every moment!

Be sincere about what you do and good things will happen. Turn the page to find out how you can find the energy to live Ageless.

The next chapter will show you how you can find the energy to move forward with your life and implement many of the changes we have discussed.

Mirror Moment

Ask yourself: *Will today be usual?* Usual hair style, usual coffeeshop espresso, and the usual people you call or text every day. Make a resolve to have an unusually great day! Gel up your hair, part it on the opposite side or swoop it up off your neck for a change. Order something different at the local hot spot that will tease your taste buds. Reach out to a long-lost friend, relative or professional and just say, "Hello, I have been thinking about you." This one simple change can make a big impact in your life—and possibly someone else's.

Chapter 7

I Have ~~No~~ Tons of Energy

During my dark years of depression and isolation, I was so exhausted that it felt like both my arms were missing. I had no desire to do anything but exist. Those negative thoughts paralyzed me at times. Even simple daily tasks seemed monumental. This may sound crazy, but I even went through a period of time where I couldn't open my mail! I allowed the mail to pile up on the kitchen table. When the pile began to topple, I'd put the mail into bags, set them aside and tell myself that I would open it all later. Later became never.

I had perfect credit until I allowed my bills to lapse. One of my credit card bills only had a charge of $50 on it, yet because I let that bill sit in the pile, unpaid for months, the card was involuntarily closed and my credit took a serious hit. It wasn't about the money; it was my mental brain fog. So many women I have met have gone through the same thing, but most of them don't want to talk about it, or don't tell anyone. It's one of those things you do not talk about, but you read about it in newspapers when the demise of someone's personal life becomes public. This type of mindset can age you fast. It can be bad for the mind and body.

Choose to Thrive

Lights, camera and NO Action! Does this sound familiar? You have zero energy for anything, even the things you used to love doing? Have you lost hope? Stopped feeling like you mattered? Become almost paralyzed by your depression?

There are several things that can throw the body into a physical shutdown, and a lot of it comes from our minds. Don't let that happen! Don't become a recluse, a prisoner in your own home, or a couch potato who binges television shows after work. I lived in the shadows myself for many years when I had lost hope and with that, my energy. I was failing to thrive because I had given up and allowed my mind and body to weaken. You have to *choose* to thrive, *choose* to live your life to the fullest. *Choose* to be ageless.

Maintain Your Energy Levels

My depression sapped my energy, and that seeped into other areas of my life. One day, I was stopped at a red light. I drifted off to sleep for a brief second. My foot must have come off the brake pedal and then…bam! My car rolled into the car in front of me, hitting the bumper of her brand-new car. I expected the other driver to yell at me, but instead, she said, "It's just a scratch". Even though she had just driven her new car off the lot, she let the moment go. I didn't. For me, that bump was a real "WAKE UP CALL!" for me to get my act together. I am thankful that it didn't take a major car accident or huge mistake to motivate me to make changes in my life. I'm sharing it with you, because I want to help you do the same.

Maintaining your energy is important. It's just as vital as making sure you have enough gas in your car before you drive across country. Energy starts, ironically, with rest. Make sure you get enough rest! Recovery sleep is an important factor in staying alert, healthy, and feeling more youthful. Bags under our eyes, droopy skin, paleness, and lack of attentiveness are telltale signs of zapped energy. If you aren't sure if you are sleeping enough, purchase one of those fitness trackers that can log your sleep at night. The one I bought had me set the right bedtime that would give me the proper amount of sleep, based on my age and gender. The tracker logged the type of sleep I was getting, whether it was deep or light, and how many times I woke up during the night. I had no idea all of this was going on while I slept. I found this information to be very helpful because I could correlate the amount of sleep I got and my performance when I was awake. I worked on improving my quality of sleep which in turn boosted my energy levels the next day.

The other important component of energy is movement. Have you ever heard of Newton's Law of Motion? *A body in motion stays in motion, a body at rest stays at rest.* To have more energy, you have to create it by turning on your body's engine and keeping it running. Start by clearing your mind, as we discussed in previous chapters, and then make a conscious effort to get moving.

Start first thing in the morning. Stretch when you wake up, then bend down and touch your toes. You may have to work at

> **ONE THING TO DO TODAY**
>
> **Plan your Energy!**
>
> By scheduling something that involves you being physical, you create an energy plan and a motivation to move. Try something like taking tennis lessons, going to a new place and meeting people, walking the dog every day. Even cleaning your house is a great activity to boost your energy and your mood. When I was in my darkest place, I wanted to pay someone to clean my house. Instead, I ended up doing it, and the sense of accomplishment was even greater than the exercise. I truly believe that doing things that create more energy contributes to my ageless living.

this daily until your fingertips reach your toes and eventually the floor. Next, reach straight up to the ceiling for a good, body-length stretch. This simple movement gets the blood flowing and turns on your engine. Inhale deep and exhale deeply a couple of times. If time permits in the morning I walk around the block, a short, five-minute walk that energizes me and wakes me up. If I do all these things, I arrive at work ready to hit the ground running. People can see my happier mood in my face and hear it in my voice. Grouchiness can come from mental and physical fatigue, lack of rest, and low energy levels. Think of it this way: Energy is happiness.

Fuel Your Energy

There is no shortage of energy foods on the market today. Power bars, power drinks, energy powders, power smoothies, power energy bowls and power meals. I am pretty sure that I have tried most all of them. Constantly filling your body with chemically processed foods, however, isn't the best choice for being ageless.

For me, I choose natural and organic foods whenever possible. I do have a few grab-and-go foods that I like when I am in a time crunch or traveling. Read the labels; know what you're eating. Look for the proper balance of proteins and carbohydrates, which can be found at the USDA's website: https://www.dietaryguidelines.gov/sites/default/files/2019-05/2015-2020_Dietary_Guidelines.pdf

Potassium is a mineral and provides electrolytes for the body, which help control the amount of water in your body, especially important for active people. To learn more about what Potassium does for the body visit: https://www.gbhealthwatch.com/Nutrient-Potassium-Overview.php I have run some 5K races, and you almost always find water and bananas for the runners to replenish them at the end. Some great natural sources of potassium are: bananas, oranges, cantaloupes, honeydew melons, apricots, grapefruit, sweet potatoes, avocado, spinach, butternut squash, and coconut water.

A lot of people reach for a cookie or candy bar in the mid-afternoon. Watch out for those sugar crashes. Even though the sugar provides a quick boost, the crash after the sugar wears off is an even bigger energy zapper. Excessive processed sugar will ramp you up high and then drop you off an energy cliff. I found this out firsthand, and much to my embarrassment, at a business luncheon. This was a working lunch where we all sat around a long conference room table and ate our meal at the same time we were conducting business. I ate two desserts because the sweet treat tasted so good. Next thing I knew, I had drifted off for a few seconds. I had my head resting on my hand, elbow on the table, and I fell asleep. Someone nudged me and the moderator joked about me having a sugar crash. Now I try to make sure that I eat healthy all the time, but especially during important functions.

Create Future Energy

Having something to look forward to is another thing that can ignite your energy, purpose, and joy. As I pulled myself out of my depression, I began to get re-involved in the things that make me happy. I started using a planner to keep track of the happenings in my life, and to make future appointments for fun. My ageless life now is far from drab and boring. I always have something to look forward to.

I am thankful that my husband encourages me to be me. You will find him behind the scenes driving me somewhere, picking me up, setting up banners and displays at my events. Look for the supporter in your life—a mate, parent, friend, or sibling—and thank them for helping you in your world and on your journey.

Remember the old me ...the women in black? My coworkers used to tease me about always wearing black. Now they say to me, "Sabrina, where are you going today? You're all dressed up!" My reply is usually some variation of, "I have my women's monthly meeting this evening/I am meeting up with a community professional/I am doing charity work." Meaning, I'm doing something I enjoy after working hours.

Music is another energizing source for me. Some of my best work is done while listening to one of my favorite songs. I can burn through a neighborhood jog with a favorite tune rocking me to the end. When I'm doing housework, I turn on one of my favorite stations and I lose track of time while I sing and clean. Have you ever been to a motivational event? The event speakers are often introduced with an empowering song. This snippet of music actually fuels the speaker so that he or she delivers a powerful presentation. One event I attended the organization played the song "Happy" after the break for lunch when people would normally be feeling drowsy. They encouraged the entire crowd of thousands to get on their feet and move with the music. Talk about waking up the audience! We all had energy to burn after that. What a brilliant idea! Can you hear the song now humming in your head?

Whenever you are struggling to get out of your doldrums, put on a song that motivates you to get up and move. Let that be your energy song that takes you from sitting to standing. Nobody has to like the song but you, because you are fueling your energy reserve, no one else's.

Sometimes you just have to push yourself to get out there and do something, even when you would rather stay inside your dark house. A few years back, my friends invited me out to karaoke. I had a million excuses not to go, but I chose to go anyway. They asked me to be a backup singer for "Rollin On the River" by Ike and Tina Turner. I was having a low-energy day, and I had never done anything like that before, but my friends pushed me and I did it. I had a blast. Your support group (I call mine my pack) can help you stay active and push you when you're feeling sluggish mentally and physically. They are your close, warm circle where you will find mutual support and affirmation. When I felt like I slowing down, being lazy or just sitting in front of the TV, munching and gaining weight, I connected with someone in my pack. Sometimes all I needed was a listening ear to help me reframe my mind, and get me out of that mood. Other times I needed a workout buddy to help get me back in shape. Within my pack we share, recipes, tips on proper eating, wellness information, and comfort. Knowing where and how to find energy and how to maintain energy will help you on your ageless journey to feeling fabulous.

For me, life is just beginning and I look forward to a new adventure each day. I have tons of energy and feel ready to make a difference wherever I can. I am so thankful that I discovered agelessness, this new way of thinking and living. These are already the very best years of my life and this book is part of me sharing with you so you too can revitalize your life.

Now that you have discovered your energy source, let's talk about how you can shape up and feel your best all the time!

Mirror Moment

If there was a dire emergency that required you to run to save your life or someone else's could you do it? That's an extreme case, but it's worth taking a hard look at where you are with your energy and your body's ability to move when needed. Start now by mentally resolving to be a body in motion. Say yes when invited to do things, especially the things that require you to leave your home.

Remember MEM: Mind-Energy-Motion.
Write it on your mirror.

Part Three

BODY MAKEOVER

Chapter 8

I'm ~~out of~~ In Shape

In my closet is a cute little blue dress that I can't bring myself to throw away. I wore it when I was twenty pounds lighter, and I don't think I'll ever get to that weight again. So why am I keeping it? From time to time, I think maybe I'll reshape my entire body to wear it again, but the fact of the matter is…that will probably never happen. If I do happen to get back to that size, it might not last for the long term. Like most of you I have had quite a roller coaster ride with my body, through all the various reasons and seasons in my life.

Blame it on Lots of Things

We all know that our genetics play a role in our body structure. For most of my teens and twenties you couldn't pour weight on me even if you tried. During my first pregnancy I had to drink shakes to make me gain weight. I only gained an extra twenty-five pounds, right up to delivery and lost most of that after giving birth to my daughter. My second child, my son, was a much bigger baby at eight pounds, two ounces, and I think giving birth to him changed my body forever. So many things affect our bodies, and we all respond differently to hormones, stress, illness, and our state of mind, both to happiness and sadness. Overeating and weight gain can be brought on my extremes in either direction.

We are uniquely made in every facet, shape, weight, and height. Even our movement, flexibility, and agility are different. We should celebrate our differences instead of trying to mold ourselves into some Hollywood ideal. The chart below is a visual expression of different physical shapes but in no way addresses our unique physical capabilities. Your body shape doesn't dictate the adventures you can have in your life.

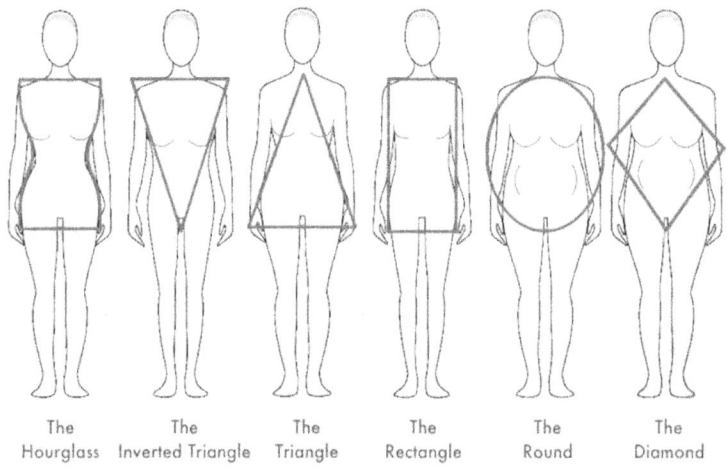

The Hourglass   The Inverted Triangle   The Triangle   The Rectangle   The Round   The Diamond

Life Brings Changes—and That's Okay

Somewhere in my late thirties I noticed a change in my physique. I had been a track star in high school so I thought, after fifteen years away from the track, I could hit the pavement and run a mile. Wrong! I huffed and puffed as I tried to carry my extra weight with my out-of-shape body. I was determined to get back in shape so I started training to run again.

The divorce had wreaked havoc on my mind and body. While going through the divorce process, I hardly ate and actually lost twenty pounds. I was skin and bones, but my body was not a healthy body. My skin was drier and my hair fell out. When I sank into a deep depression, I slid to the opposite end of the spectrum and gained thirty pounds. I was hiding it all in black clothes, or so I thought. I had let myself go during that time, in more ways than one. The mind has so much control over the body. Have you had times in your life where what you were going through affected your weight? I bet you have, just as I have.

Know How Healthy You Are

It might be hard to believe but I allowed seven years to slip by without going for a physical or my annual women care visit. I am an educated woman and I knew better, but allowed that depression to rule my life. My mother kept telling me I needed to go to the doctor so I could establish a baseline for my health. I argued that I felt fine, even though I was overweight for my body type. I finally listened to her and scheduled a wellness visit with a naturopathic doctor.

When I was there, I had to step on a scale and face reality. When my bloodwork came back I got another shock. I was pre-diabetic, low in vitamin D3, and low in vitamin B12. The doctor asked me

WHAT TYPE OF TRAINING IS RIGHT FOR YOU?

Here are two options, and some points to remember for each:

Certified Personal Trainer:

- Can be a coach/mentor client/goal setter
- Has knowledge of body composition
- Has knowledge of muscles
- Has knowledge of body limitations
- Has knowledge of nutrition
- Has knowledge of proper handling of equipment, weights, pulleys
- Can do a fitness assessment to determine strengths/weaknesses

Independent Training/Home Gym

- No accountability
- No mentor motivation
- May set weak goals
- May lack knowledge of nutrition
- May have limited knowledge of proper handling of fitness equipment: weights, pulleys, resistance bands
- Hard to do a personal assessment
- Hard to stay consistent

if I exercised and told me I needed to keep it movin'. Either make my body more active or go on prescriptions meds. My body was telling me it was out of kilter with weight gain, but I wasn't listening. Getting back on track was a simple fix. I started walking fifteen to twenty minutes a day to keep the diabetes in check. The doctor asked me to come back in three months.

I was determined not to go on prescription medications, so I took the doctor's advice. I thought no one noticed the extra pounds in my black clothes, but when I had lost twelve pounds before that next doctor's visit, one of my friends said, "I see you got that weight off of you." My doctor was pleased with my progress and so was I. It was the first step toward a new ageless and healthy future.

Have you ignored the warning signs of your body? Have you stopped caring for yourself like I did? It's easy to do when life hands you a blow or when you are feeling lost, lonely, rejected or look in the mirror and think you are losing that youthful luster. It's never too late to make a change. I am living proof of what a few simple changes can do.

Know What Your Body Can Do

Even though I had lost weight, I was not in shape. I couldn't touch my toes and couldn't run without getting winded. I joined a gym to help me get my body back to being ageless—meaning reaching my physical potential, not trying to become a twenty-year-old again. When I commit to something, I go all the way, and knew I needed support. I convinced a friend of mine to sign up as a workout buddy. We took Before pictures to remind us of what we looked like. I must tell you, they were not pretty pictures. We hid our pictures in our phones in a special folder for our viewing only.

I remember I couldn't even touch my toes because my middle had too much middle in it. There was so much I could not do when I enrolled in this class. My gym time was 5:00 am for one hour five days a week and sometime six to seven days if I was on a roll. After my workout, I would come home, shower, take a twenty-minute power nap and headed out the door for work by 7:30 am. I took it slow and learned to respect the equipment, weights, pulleys, rowing machines, and treadmill. We had a group personal trainer for a class of about twenty people so there was adequate supervision. I highly recommend that you get a personal trainer or some kind of assistance if you are going to start up a new, strenuous high-impact fitness program after being sedentary for a while. You can injure yourself easily, thinking you can do more than your body is ready to do. Low-impact home exercises like walking, swimming, and stretching are not too much of a concern unless you have pre-existing health conditions. As always, check with your doctor before starting any new fitness program.

Set Goals and Keep Track

My fitness tracker told me my level of fitness each day and how many calories I was burning. To really stay on top of what I was putting into my body, I logged my meals each day and installed a free app called myfitnesspal. This is a great app because you can scan barcodes to add food, set a calorie and/or weight goal, add your fitness activities, manage your weight, and get healthy recipes. It syncs with many trackers like an Apple watch or Fitbit. After about six months, I was in my best shape ever post-divorce. Touching my toes, ramping up the treadmill,

> **DO ONE THING TODAY**
>
> Pick one fitness activity that you can do to add movement to your day. Whether it's dancing to music, taking a walk, or going to the gym, ten to fifteen minutes a day is all you need to start shaping up.

and maintaining endurance on the rowing machine proved to me that our bodies can regain vitality, even as we mature.

For a number of years in that gym I held the women's record for a four-minute plank, enduring longer than women twenty to twenty-five years younger than me. Age was not a factor; it was my mind, my willpower, and my desire to be ageless among my peers. The more I went to the gym, the more my body and agility improved. Remember the secret pictures hidden in my phone? One time, I accidently scrolled past them in front of someone. I was embarrassed, but also proud of how far I had come.

Be realistic about your goals, where you are in life, and your overall health. My shape continues to change as I mature, just like my hair, eyesight, skin tone, and nails. Ageless is my goal, meaning, achieving the best body by doing the best that I can. Today, you will find me being active at home. I walk a block, then run a block with my favorite tunes playing for a total of two miles. After that I coast back home with another two-mile walk at my pace. All in all, I do about 10,000 steps per day, at least three days per week. My husband built me a home gym and equipped it with a treadmill, abdominal machine, weights, and resistance bands. Over the years I have learned to pace myself and how to safely handle weights. Every now

---

LOW IMPACT VERSUS HIGH IMPACT EXERCISES – WHICH IS BETTER FOR YOU?

Low Impact Exercises

Easy on the joints. Options include walking, gentle stretching, cycling, swimming. Low impact is great for beginners, those with injuries, or medical conditions.

High Impact Exercises

Tougher/Harder on joints. Options include running, jumping, bouncing, strenuous. Places exertion on the body.

* Always get a doctor's recommendation first to determine what is appropriate for your body and overall health.

and then I will engage a personal trainer for a few months to round out my workouts.

Whether you choose a gym, personal trainer, or a home workout, remember your footwear and clothing contribute to your workout performance. Walking shoes are not running shoes. There is a difference, so make sure you read up on them before you make a purchase, or go to a running shoe store because they will do a gait analysis to see what will suit you best. I always go a half size up in my workout footwear to allow room for my socks and so that my toes are not crunched. If you are lifting weights, wear gloves for that purpose. You can find a good pair in most discount stores in the sporting goods section. Wear workout clothes that allow you to breathe and that are not too constricting. I was always taught "Form Follows Function," meaning cute and pretty gym clothes are less important than how you will move and workout in those clothes.

If you need a little help getting started, check out my **Ageless Techniques 30 Day Fit & Healthy Jump Start Program,** which can be found on my website. This program includes simple meal choices, shopping tips, and easy-to-do fitness activities for at home.

Try Creative Options

You don't have to go to a gym to get exercise. Try something fun, like dancing. My husband and I love to dance. We are the first ones on the dance floor at wedding receptions, a social gathering, or an evening out where there is good food and a nice band. Dancing elevates the heart rate and stretches the muscles. If you come to my house while I'm doing housework, you'll find a little music going, and see me stop once in a while to get few dance moves in. What about you? If you want to start moving more, try putting on some tunes while you work at home and see what happens. I feel like a teenager when I'm dancing and you will too. Being ageless is fun!

Once you commit to getting your body in shape and maintaining it you will find that you have more energy. Keeping up with my active lifestyle is only possible because of my fitness program, and vice versa. It's a wonderful, interconnected concept!

Staying physically active is also supported by living healthy. Check out my Webinar on Fitness for more of my personal tips. Turn the page to find out ways to round out your ageless lifestyle!

Mirror Moment

Are you shaped or shapeless? Be honest. Do you get winded exerting yourself? Are your clothes shrinking in the dryer or are you expanding a bit? These are tough questions, but the answers could save your life. Being active promotes a healthy heart and overall strong body. According to the Harvard Medical School, regular exercise can add years to your life. (*Harvard Health Letter*, Published: February 2013)

Chapter 9

I'm ~~on a Diet~~ Living Healthy

Mirror, Mirror on the wall, who's the thinnest of them all? So many of us worry about our weight and how thin we are, or how thin we used to be. Before kids I was a size zero, but I didn't stay that way. Like I mentioned earlier our bodies are constantly changing, and that's okay because it's part of the life cycle. The problem is most women can't accept their weight and are on perpetual diets, to try and get even thinner. Why do we all want to be as thin as rails? Are we trying to copy some magazine-cover/Hollywood ideal that is impossible to attain? Is it because those images and that body takes us back to our young adulthood when were in our prime? AKA, "our best years"? For most of us, when we were eighteen to twenty-five, our hair was longer, our bones were stronger, our skin was firmer, and our muscles were toner. You can't turn back the clock on your age—but you can change the future and create a body that gives you joy, and that will last a lifetime.

Mental Weight is Heavy

I didn't just have physical weight gain—I had mental weight, too. My mental weight became a problem for me when I was going through my divorce and the ensuing isolation years. At first my mind would not allow me to eat because all I could do was think about separating my family, losing my husband,

and becoming a single parent. Maybe because I felt like I failed or I was somehow unworthy? Even when I ate my food was tasteless.

I always made sure that the kids ate good meals, and I would sit with them while they ate, but I picked at my food. We had a custody arrangement with the children so on my off weekend, things got really bad. Dead silence in my home and no reason to cook. All I did was lie around the house in front of the television or stay in bed, feeling sorry for myself. When I did eat, I never chose healthy food. As I became less active, I started to gain weight, and my mind kept me in that unhealthy cycle for far too long.

This is how powerful the mind can be. All of these thoughts, and the weight gain that accompanied them, contributed to my lack of self-esteem and feeling unwanted, old, and now overweight. I was dressing frumpy, in oversized, black clothes. I was not in a good place. Have you been through something like this, where you self-inflicted pain and weight, due to your mental anxiety? Many of us do, and for some of us, we need medical help or prescription drugs to help cope. There is no shame in getting the help you need, so if you are feeling depressed or hopeless, call a doctor, please.

When I adapted my new ageless thinking, I went back mentally to the secrets for healthy living that I'd lived before. Back to when I was the perfect size and felt good about myself. Not the perfect size by some magazine's standards, but by my own, because that was the size where I felt my best, physically and mentally. I started reading up on nutrition, and fitness, and how the two worked together. I was able to find myself again and get my body back. Because I want the same for you, I'll share what I discovered and my journey to this new better place. Are you ready?

Planned Meals Means Planned Success

When I was growing up, we never heard much about diets in our home. We lived in the South and that meant Sunday dinner was comprised of homemade *everything*. We were a family of five: Mom, Dad, me and my two siblings. Mom expected us to help prepare dinner which included peeling potatoes, cutting up celery, and boiling eggs for her signature potato salad. Our favorite meal was southern fried chicken, mashed potatoes and gravy, corn bread, and collard greens. Oh yes, and don't forget the fresh sweet potato pie right out of the oven for dinner. We ate homemade pancakes for breakfast complete with eggs and bacon. We ate a lot of farm-grown fruits and veggies like melons, citrus, squash, field peas, tomatoes, peppers, black eyed peas, corn, and okra. We drove to a place called Murphy groves and picked out bushel fruits and vegetable. A favorite family past-time was shucking corn and shelling field peas on a lazy Sunday afternoon. Fast food places were just starting to pop up, but this was not a choice for our family. Maybe once or twice a year my dad would take the family out to a nice sit-down restaurant as a treat. Despite all that homemade goodness, none of us were overweight. What about you? Did you eat more home-cooked meals as a kid?

When I married and had children, I initially kept up the tradition of home cooking until our schedules became more complex. I had never had boxed mashed potatoes before, but I found myself trying them, along with other prepared foods because our lives were so hectic and time to cook was minimal. Next thing I knew, I was buying boxed everything. It seemed so innovative at the time. We got caught up in processed food. Don't get me wrong, it never tasted as good as mom's southern cooking, but it was quick and easy. We started patronizing fast food places and ordering the kid's meals, complete with burger, fries, drink, and a toy! How healthy was that?

Looking back, I can see where I made some poor food choices by getting caught up in quick fixes. Life is about balance, as I have stated before. There are times where you only have five minutes to eat and you might have to grab a quick something. Just don't make it an everyday habit.

Our daily planned meals should be just that, planned. This is where healthy living starts. My mother prepared a grocery list before she went shopping. She knew the meals she would prepare for the week. She had, in essence, a plan. I had to break the bad habits I had developed of running to the grocery store on a whim, picking up whatever things caught my eye, and figuring out meals while I shopped. I wasted so much money doing that. Sometimes I purchased items I already had at home. I am reformed now and know exactly what I need for the week and only make one shopping trip. My husband prefers home cooking over restaurant food and so do I. Since we are a family of two now, we balance cooking at home with eating out. As a rule of thumb, we try to make healthy menu item choices when we eat out, but every now and then we eat something decadent. Ageless means having that piece of cake as a treat just as you did when you were in your twenties—but not making cake a meal. You must be honest with yourself if you want this to work.

Pick the Right Eating Style

Before I got back into home cooking, I tried every diet under the sun. The rice diet, which consisted of eating bland rice and rice cakes, no condiments, or seasonings allowed for two or three weeks. All I know is, yes, I lost weight, but I doubled over in stomach pains when I introduced mustard, ketchup, salt, and pepper back into my body. It was horrible. Be careful with fad diets. Not all diets are bad; some are good, effective and necessary for certain health conditions. However, healthy meals may eliminate the need for dieting if done with the proper balance of food groups, along with moderate exercise.

Intermittent fasting is another method of limiting calorie intake and boosting your metabolism. Fasting has been around for centuries. Intermittent fasting consists of confining your meals to an eight-hour window and then fasting for the remaining sixteen hours. For the past year I have doing intermittent fasting and incorporating this program in with healthy meal choices. It works for me, but please note, I am not recommending any particular type of diet program for you, but rather more of a focus on healthier food choices. Always consult with your doctor on any changes in your food regimen. Remember, I am pre-diabetic so my food and fitness choices may differ from yours.

Drinking water plays a major role in our body care. Personally, I drink eight glasses of water per day. I keep bottled water at my desk and will consume two sixteen-ounce bottles by 5 pm. I also carry a bottle of water with me at all times. By the end of the evening I have consumed another bottle of water with dinner and one just before bedtime. This system might be helpful (and healthful) if you struggle with getting all of your glasses of water in for the day. You may also add a little twist of lemon in your water if you need to boost up the taste a bit. I have eliminated sodas from my diet and only consume them on special occasions.

Do you like smoothies? A smoothie can be the perfect on-the-go drink packed with fruits, veggies and protein. Try making yours at home for better quality. I prepare mine the night before and refrigerate them for a grab-and-go breakfast. Use fresh fruits and veggies like strawberries, bananas, spinach, and carrots. You may freeze these and throw them right in your blender eliminating the need to add ice to your smoothie. There are various ways to add protein to your drink including whey, plants and dairy. These drinks are not calorie-free so keep this in mind if you are watching your caloric intake. If you prefer a sweeter taste, add some honey. Remember the goal is healthy and clean eating whenever possible.

The Sugar and Snack Dilemma

Do you have a sweet tooth? Sugary foods and sweeteners can be a challenge for healthy living. The supermarket carries a variety of refined sugars, raw sugars, and artificial sugar choices with pros and cons that can be quite confusing. If you have health conditions you will want to do your own research to find out which is the best option for you.

I am very selective about consuming sugary foods. Of course I'll eat a cookie on occasion just because, but it's not part of my daily consumption. Read labels carefully because sugar is an ingredient in a lot of processed foods. On food labels sugar masquerades under different names such as, sucrose, glucose, maltose, dextrose, high fructose corn syrup, cane syrup, concentrated fruit juice, honey, and agave nectar.

Energy drinks are also popular today. Some brands are loaded with sugar so again educate yourself and know what you are consuming. Are you a coffee drinker? Try cutting back on the sugar in your coffee one teaspoon at time until your taste buds adapt to the new taste. I attribute my overall well-being and healthy weight to cutting back on sweet things.

Snacking can lead to you packing on undesirable pounds. For the best option, I go back to my childhood on this one. When we said to Mother after dinner that we were hungry she told us to eat a piece of fruit. We were taught to eat whole foods back then. My grandmother lived two blocks away from us and her yard was loaded with fruit trees: mango, orange, pink meat grapefruit, lemons, and limes. We would walk down to her house and pick the low-hanging fruit. We learned to climb the trees and use a pole to get the fruit, too. We learned how to cut up whole watermelon and eat right off the rind. We also enjoyed cantaloupe and honeydew melons. My dad even taught us how to open a coconut. As kids we ate whole, healthy, natural foods—and those are the best snacks. Try fruits or things like carrot sticks, celery sticks, broccoli, cauliflower, sliced tomatoes, and sliced peppers. I try to keep these items in stock at home so that I am not tempted to eat processed food. My weakness is popcorn and barbeque-flavored potato chips. I have to fess up on that. What about you?

What we were doing back then was essentially eating organic. To me, that means whole food ingredients. When I purchase food with an Organic label, I look for the words "certified organic". This helps me stick with healthier choices overall. I like shopping in organic food stores even though the prices are a little higher, because I know the foods are often healthier. If you are buying fruits and veggies with a skin on them the product is already naturally protected so you may not need to select organic. For leafy produce which is often exposed to chemicals and insecticides, opt for organic. When in doubt, ask your grocer or a local organic farmer.

Subscription Meal Services

If you want to eat healthy and have very little time, there are meal subscription services available that help you cut down the prep time. These services offer whole meals portioned out for each serving, and contain all the ingredients necessary to plate the dish. This is a pay-by-subscription service so you have to be willing to receive so many meals per week for a certain price. Some offer organic meals, which is a plus. Research the services carefully and know the pros and cons before signing up.

The Prescription is Easy

In a nutshell, my discovery to healthy living was old-school eating and remaining physically active. Whether you are a meat eater or a vegetarian, eating fresh whole foods and lean meats cooked at home is better for you, just like my mother taught us. Even if you are a single person you can prepare your foods ahead of time and freeze them. When I was single, I purchased single serving plasticware to use for meal prepping. This way you control the portion size and the quality of the meal.

Another big key to living healthy is having positive thoughts. I keep a healthy mind by not filling it up with negative data. I do not circulate nor do I like to receive distressful information. This is not to say that I am unplugged from world events; it means that I choose not to entertain recurring thoughts about things that I do not have the power to change.

> **ONE THING TO DO TODAY**
>
> You don't have to swap out all your meals at once. Start small, with one meal at a time. Even reducing your sugar intake is a great beginning. Experiment with adding in new or organic foods. One step leads to the next!

I keep my mental side on track and living ageless by finding enjoyment in nature. My husband and I both love the beach life. This is where we both find our inner peace and happiness. The décor of our home is coastal living to remind us of our favorite place when we aren't there. We love going to the beach, hearing the sound of the ocean, and smelling the salty air as it rolls off the waves. The sand between my toes grounds me to the earth and the cool salt water running over my feet is like being in a whirlpool. A healthy and happy mind contributes to a healthy body, so find your healthy place and visit it often.

Now that you are on board with living healthy, turn the page to pull everything together in our All-Over Makeover.

Mirror Moment

Is the real you just pounds away? Have you allowed yourself to get to a bad place that has affected your overall wellness and wellbeing?

Today, decide to take your life back and reprogram your thinking on your food choices. Make a grocery list of healthy foods you would like to have at home, some for snacks and some for home cooking. Once the ball is in motion and the food is at your fingertips you will start enjoying better meals. Make it easy on yourself to make a change!

Chapter 10

The All-Over Make Over

When I graduated high school, I had been homecoming queen, and thought the world ahead would be bright and beautiful. I went through a myriad of changes in the years since then: marriage, kids, divorce, single life, and then a wonderful second marriage. My weight had been up and down, my clothes went from drab to colorful, and my mental state fluctuated through all those life changes. When I latched onto and decided to live the ageless life, however, all of that changed. My outlook brightened, and I saw the journey I went through as a necessary part that brought me to where I was today.

Still, I was nervous when my husband and I attended my forty-year high school class reunion. Everyone wanted to know what the homecoming queen looked like today. I was so happy, and so proud, of the transformation I had gone through. Everyone welcomed me with open arms, commenting that I looked great! I have to admit, that was a scary door to walk through. There was a little fear of not living up to their expectations, and that tiny bit of insecurity we all have from time to time. (A quick shoutout to my class: GO GREEN WAVE! Fort Myers High School Class of 76!)

When I was at the reunion, dozens of people asked me about why I looked so healthy and happy. I was thrilled to share my ageless journey that started inside my mind, rebuilt my self, and strengthened my body. I'm hoping this book can help you get to that place that makes you feel good about yourself, that place where your self-esteem is high and when you walk into a room you do so with confidence and strength. Growing Ageless paves the way for a renewed, stronger you.

Think Young, Live Younger

Think young, live younger is the motto I live by. In this book, we have talked about how much of our interpretation of who and what we are resides in the recesses our minds. Instead of focusing on a number on a scale or on my driver's license, I had to allow myself to see the younger version of me. Growing ageless involved a self-assessment of Sabrina:

Who is she?

What is she all about?

What does she want to do moving forward?

To answer those questions for me and for you:

1. I am a woman who still wants to enjoy life.
2. I love helping people and I want to feel good about the legacy that I am creating.
3. I hope that my passion for living an active lifestyle, mentoring others and leading the way to living ageless will inspire and educate other women now and in the future.

Before you can move forward from aging to ageless you must answer these same three questions. Take out a pad of paper and take your time answering them, because these answers are the key to your future. The words will be the essence of you and what you want, not what someone else wants you to be. With these answers, you are creating your very own unique roadmap to discovering the life-changing world of agelessness!

I have termed this new class of men and women, those of you reading this book and celebrating life, as the Ageless Generation. Can't you just feel the energy and exhilaration lifting off these pages and into your mind? I get excited thinking about it, talking about it, writing about it, and sharing this mindset with groups of people.

> **SIGNS OF AGING**
>
> - Lack of physical energy
> - Lack of mental sharpness (sometimes called a brain fog)
> - Poor sleeping patterns
> - Poor eating habits
> - Thinning, fragile hair
> - Sagging body, less muscle tone, stiffness
> - Dry skin, less elastic

Take a Good Look in the Mental Mirror

In this book, we've had a "Mirror Moment" in every chapter, as a chance for you to look in your mental mirror and be honest with yourself. Most of us are forgiving of what we see when we look in the regular mirror. We see a thick waist or a few pounds in the thighs, and give ourselves grace before we do something about it, by choosing flattering outfits or heading to the gym.

> For more information, check out my webinars on my website:
>
> - Wellness to Ageless
> - Fitness to Ageless
> - Dancing to Ageless

Your mental mirror is there for self-analysis. My mirror told me that my head was not right and neither was my body. Depression, hair loss, extra weight, feelings of failure—all those things were haunting me. They were also aging me, and sucking the life out of my life. If you are feeling the same, here are some signs and solutions that should help with your ageless makeover.

Great Hair Tips

This book has already talked about the mental and self changes you can make to be more ageless. Let's talk about hair for a moment, because our appearance can affect our mood and our ageless attitude whether we like it or not. When we were younger most of us had so much hair that we tried thinning it out with special combs, cutting it, and perming it to keep it under control. My hair was long and thick, so I added a chemical relaxer to keep it under control. I also loved coloring my hair so it was always a reddish brown or golden brunette. I never thought I would see the day when my hair would fall out or break easily. Depression and stress affected both the inside and the outside of my head. Once I found clarity in my life, my hair began to grow back and feel healthier. My hair now is not as thick as it was in my youth, but that's okay because I've found ways to enhance my hair with dark brown extensions. I'm all about being real and honest, and admitting that every once in a while, there's a little extra something that helps me to keep looking and growing ageless.

> **SOLUTIONS: HAIR AND SCALP – THINNING AND POOR QUALITY**
>
> - Check your hormone levels and/or have a physical at the doctor's office
> - Lower the stress levels in your life, mind and body
> - Maintain a clean scalp and hair, using quality products

Great Body Tips

The human body has a great renewal design. We injure ourselves, and the body works to repair and heal the wound. Our body is a gift that must be cherished and taken care of regardless of our age. We can assist the body in retaining a measure of vitality, if we listen to what our bodies tell us. When you are imbalanced physically or sick, your body will tell you. If you are stressed or depressed, your body will show signs of it. You can turn things around and restore your vitality if you listen and respond. I am happy that no permanent damage was done to my body while I was in that dark time in my life. I was determined to never be there again.

I'm not going to say that getting back in shape was easy. There were plenty of moans and groans when I worked with my personal trainer. She showed no mercy and she knew I could do more, so she pushed me within my limits. I remember her checking my abs each time I went for a workout to be sure I was doing my "homework". That kept me accountable and gave me a goal to shoot for. Make a resolution to be active on a regular basis and you will see results. Are you willing to put in the work? If so, set your realistic goals and start moving! My goal was not a number on the scale, it was a dress size. Now I can gauge my body by how well my clothes fit. Find what works best for you and stick to it. Ageless is healthy, toned and fit.

> **SOLUTIONS – REGAINING OUR AGELESS BODY**
>
> - Eat a balanced diet rich in antioxidants
> - Get proper hydration (drink adequate water)
> - Stay active; movement gains back years

Eating a balanced diet impacts our mind, body, skin, and hair. You are what you eat, as the saying goes, and it's true. Pick a meal plan that is realistic for you. You'll find plenty of options, ranging from ketogenic to Mediterranean and vegetarian. Mediterranean is one of my favorites, because it is full of healthy vegetables and light, satisfying meals. As I stated in the previous chapter, opt for fresh, whole foods whenever possible. Choosing home cooking over processed foods had a big impact on my body and on slimming down. Losing weight makes you look more youthful and ageless. Don't forget to also drink plenty of water as part of your daily regime. Our mission is transformation into an ageless body, one that will make you smile when you look in the mirror.

Great Skin Tips

Our skin is our largest organ, and because of that, it's an open testimony about our overall wellness. When we meet people, it is that face-to-face experience that leads us to make initial assessments about their age. We identify them as teenagers, young adults, mature adults, or seniors. I never tell people my age unless they ask, and many people are surprised at how old I am, because my skin looks great and ageless.

Taking care of your skin is a must-do for looking ageless. Over time your skin will start to show a little wear and tear but there are some things you can do to keep it healthier looking, namely: reduce stress, keep it clean and hydrated. My daily skincare regimen consists of a facial cleanser, toner, and a moisturizing anti-aging cream before bed and again when I wake up each morning. I drink a lot of water and try to keep my stress at a minimum. I attribute this system to my healthy, youthful, toned skin. For more information on my skincare system, visit my website, www.agelesstechniques.com.

> **SOLUTIONS: AGING TO AGELESS SKIN**
>
> - Protect the skin from the sun
> - Moisturize daily
> - Get adequate sleep

General Ageless Tips

Your smile is everything. That means that we have to take care of our teeth. I made the decision to get braces in my forties. My bite was not that bad but I had one front tooth that protruded further than the others. The braces were a personal gift to myself that made me feel good. I still see my dentist annually for cleaning, and to take care of any issues before they get out of hand. This is another example of you taking a personal self-examination to see where you can make improvements that will get you back to looking ageless.

Your eyes are another attractive feature of the total you. My eyes are brown but they were hidden behind glasses for years. I now wear bifocal contact lenses. Like everything else, our vision changes as we move through the cycle of life. If you can't wear contacts, look for some nice, modern, chic frames. This is another way to add a little spark to your appearance.

The way we carry ourselves and interact with others is also part of the ageless makeover. Take some pride in the way you sit, walk, and stand. Unless you have health issues, refrain from slouching in chairs and dragging your feet when you walk. Look alert and interested, not sad and droopy. Would you purchase a flower that is starting to wilt or would you pick one that stands up straight and is vibrant and colorful? This is all part of the vibe that we transmit to others, and which speaks volumes about whether you are aging or ageless.

In conversations, speak clearly and concisely. Hold your head up as you speak, and be sure to smile because it makes a big difference in your tone and demeanor. Recently, I received an award for delivering a presentation before a group of professional women. I was honored to know that I can still motivate people during this ageless time in my life. You can too!

The final touches on our growing ageless journey is our decorum. I had to ditch the black clothes

ONE THING TO DO TODAY

Take a piece of paper and draw a line down the middle. On one side of the line write the word NOW and on the other side of the paper write the words IN PROGRESS.

Under the NOW column write down the things we have discussed in this chapter that are quick fixes. Under the IN PROGRESS column write down the things that will take a little bit of transformation time. I don't use words like long-term because those are back burner terms that encourage you to procrastinate. I want you to move forward with intention so that you can reap the benefits of growing ageless sooner rather than later!

and now I live in winter and spring colors. I look good in papaya, deep peaches, greens, fuchsia, and royal blues. Do you know what your color season is or what colors look good on you? These colors should bring out the vibrant hues in your skin. When I was in my twenties, I did color draping to find the perfect colors for me and my skin tone. You can find your color chart at: https://www.colormebeautiful.com/seasons/findyourseason.html. Knowing your colors can help you put together a winning wardrobe that will enhance your look and make you appear more approachable and professional, perfect for when you expand your connections.

Revamping your closet does not have to be expensive. Bargain shop to find the best values. Look for styles that fit your personality. I prefer a classy and sophisticated look; others might want something fun and funky. Dress up your outfit with a pair of heels if you are physically able to wear them. My footwear of choice is platform heels because they give the appearance of stilettos but keep your feet at a more comfortable angle. Whatever your personal look is, always show up looking your best. Have fun implementing your colors and selecting fashionable styles to enhance the beautiful person that you are.

When you are living in a world of ageless, one thing to remember—there are no numbers allowed. Age doesn't matter. Weight doesn't matter. Ageless living is about getting the most life out of your life! Have gratitude and a positive attitude, and you will find that ageless attitude bringing you a renewed, life-lasting peace and happiness!

Mirror Moment

This is your time to look at the whole person of you in the mirror. Who do you see? Someone who is happy? Sad? Someone who has allowed herself or himself to age faster?

Right now is the moment to take control of your life, your mind, your body, and your persona. It's time to reshape you and grow ageless.

Look at that reflection and say to yourself: It's time to start my ageless journey. I have so many more years to enjoy life to the fullest and I intend to joyfully live every single one of them!

About Women's Entrepreneurial Empowerment (W.E.E.)

W.E.E. was founded in November 2016 by Sabrina Protic. After attending numerous networking meet-ups, Sabrina decided to start an organization that would help women entrepreneurs gain visibility and traction in their businesses. Today, W.E.E conducts monthly meeting with guest speakers who deliver enlightened information for personal and professional development. W.E.E. also hosts yearly events that showcase women entrepreneurs and support the community.

Vision: Women's Entrepreneurial Empowerment will share a vital role in maintaining an endless circle of connectivity and exposure within the consumer and professional ranks.

Mission: Women's Entrepreneurial Empowerment strives for continuous opportunities for women to expand their networks, develop relationships, and grow their businesses. We empower and support women entrepreneurs via personal and professional education, strategic business information, and engaging in community enrichment.

Values: Women's Entrepreneurial Empowerment embraces the following guiding principles: Inspiration, Integrity, Diversity, Excellence, and Innovation.

For more information:

https://www.wee-womenentrepreneurs.com/

Email:Admin@wee-womenentrepreneurs.com

FB Page @wee-womenentrepreneurs

Instagram @wee-womenentrepreneurs

Exposure Fuels Growth – Sabrina Protic

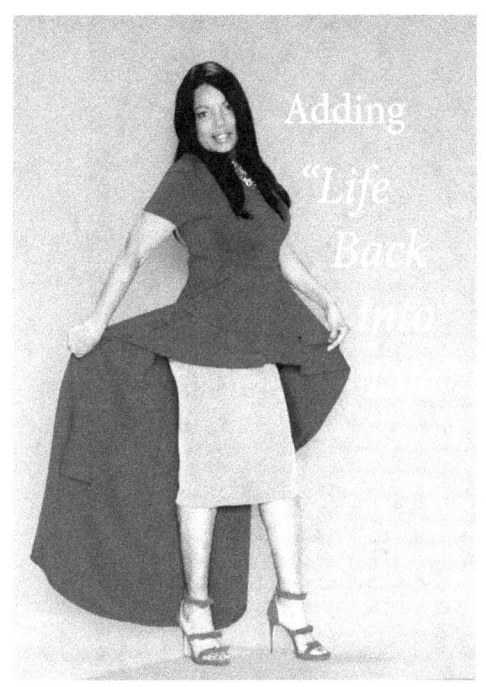

Adding "Life Back Into

Dancing is a creative option for spicing up your level of movement and activity.

My Black Wardrobe

Diving lessons. Step out of your comfort zone

AgelessTechniques.com

Good skincare regime promotes ageless skin

Speaking and hosting events

Inner peace at the beach for us promotes a happy and healthy mind

Taking the time to be productive and build roadmaps to inspire others

Mindset Reset

Active is moving…enjoy walking anytime, anywhere, on the treadmill, on the pavement or in the park.

Aged   **Ageless**

About the Author

Sabrina Protic is an energetic and vibrant wife, mother, grandmother, career professional, entrepreneur, and certified life coach. Her passion is to help others who have gone through life-changing setbacks and give them the tools to overcome by adding "Life Back into Life". Wherever she goes, she shares her journey and how she conquered depression, loneliness, isolation, and the almost-crippling feelings of being too old to find happiness again.

Sabrina founded Ageless Techniques to promote a healthier mind/body and more youthful, energized, and active way of life. She has always had a fascination with maintaining vitality through natural approaches to wellness including, diet, fitness, and herbs. You will find Sabrina being active in the community, speaking, and leading her women's empowerment organization, W.E.E.

"Adding Life Back into Life"

Contact Sabrina here:

FB: @AgelessTechniques.com

FB: @DiscoverAgeless

Instagram: @DiscoverAgeless

Email: Younger@agelesstechniques.com

www.ingramcontent.com/pod-product-compliance
Lightning Source LLC
Chambersburg PA
CBHW052100070526
44584CB00017B/2268